ARGENTINE
WINE

A PRACTICAL HANDBOOK

ARGENTINE WINE

A PRACTICAL HANDBOOK

Jorge Dengis - María Fernanda Dengis

CONTENTS

Foreword 6
Argentine Wine, a Practical Handbook 8
A great challenge 9

CHAPTER 1
Wine as ever 11
A ride through History 13
The making of wine 16
Red wine vinification 18
White wine vinification 20

CHAPTER 2
Argentina, a wine-bearing country 23
A history of wine in Argentina 25
Argentine wine 26
Exporting Argentina 28
Wine-bearing regions 30
The most used varieties in Argentina 34
Generic or blend wines 42
Varietal wines and the Californian "revolution" 44

CHAPTER 3
Wine tasting 49
Sampling: a game for training wine-tasters 51
Tasting 54
Art not science 56
Colour 58
Aroma 60
Taste 62
How should a wine be drunk for proper tasting? 64

CHAPTER 4
Of pleasures and ceremonies 67
Nobody drinks the same wine twice 69

Wine and language 72
Of glasses and temperatures 74
The label, wine's visiting card 78
The cork 82
Wine accessories 86
Matching between wine and food 90
How to set up your own cellar 94

CHAPTER 5
Champagne, the prince of wines 97
An exquisite and singular beverage 99
Traditional champagne 99
Method for exclusive champagne 100
Argentine champagne 102
How to taste sparkling wine? 103

CHAPTER 6
Wine world: price and quality 105
Denomination of origin 107
The unavoidable price/quality ratio 110
The leading role of liquor stores 112
Interview with Daniel Dengis 114

APPENDIX
Frequently-asked questions 117
Everything about wines 119
Brief enological dictionary 123

WINE COMPANIES IN ARGENTINA 129
Boutique companies 131
Others producers 188
Index of wine cellars 190

Foreword

The author of the wisest and most captivating work ever written on the sensory characteristics of wine addresses his readers to remind them that, if they are from a country of renowned winemaking tradition they are direct heirs to the civilization of wine. They may also belong in a place recently colonized by grapevine, but even in this latter case, it is simultaneously a representative and a responsible for the quality of wine.

This because it's certainly up to the consumer of a wine to consecrate its quality, the more demanding desires and refined taste, the more concrete and real the quality of wine offered by the producer to please him or her.

From the beginning the reputation of certain wines —today a part of the cultural patrimony of countries or regions where they have arrived— is one of the most representative expressions of the degree of civilization achieved by humankind in its day.

Demands concerning wine quality are relatively easily defined, which doesn't amount to a corresponding feasibility of their achievement.

According to renowned wine lover Jean Onizet, the author of a prolific literary work on wine and its qualities, it takes a madman to grow the grapevine, a wise man to rule it; a lucid artist to vinify and a passionate amateur to drink.

Bizarre lyricism aside, it can be said that wine is the result of a varied, complex set of natural and human factors that must be harmoniously matched to make a product of recognized excellence.

This way every wine —even those made of a single variety of *Vitis vinifera*— will be the consequence of the vinification of a harvest conditioned by a given *terroir* with a nature, i.e. soil and climate confer it a particular composition, to which man-made culture works add up. Every year this gives peculiar characteristics to harvests reaching the cellars and the enologists subjects to the process of original vinification and handling. This way, a diversity of oenological processes is added to the wide range of grapevine varieties, multiplicity of *terroirs* and culture work plus the seasonal imprint, giving the wine particular characteristics typical from every vintage.

A great number of new producers have been emerging lately in the best part of wine-producing countries, Argentina an outstanding case among these. Indeed, we could observe an enormous quantity of new wines, some from well-known producers but also —better, especially— others from new companies, many small and from new areas. Most of these have the great ambition of achieving high-quality wines, moreover the big challenge of conquering the most demanding markets as well as the recognition and image of great wines.

In view of such a profuse production we are surprised by the extension and orderliness of the description of the huge vinicultural production, accompanied by gorgeous pictures, carried out by the authors of *Argentine Wine. A Practical Handbook*. This is a valuable contribution to the knowledge-thirsty reader who will be solvently illustrated on the rich palette of wines available in the marketplace.

Roberto de la Mota

Argentine Wine, a Practical Handbook

The author of this book started to get interested in wines at the age of twenty. In 1951 I became a journalist and I was invited to take part in a very interesting editorial project: the gestation of *El economista*, an economical-financial weekly publication still in the business in spite of the Cassandras who tried to discourage us back then by arguing that economical opinion was a subject reserved to a few. I accepted a three-month training period and worked there for almost twenty years. Shortly after I became a Senior Editor, then General Secretary .

In the early 1960s a workmate and I came out with the idea of including in every issue a small gastronomic section which, according to our intuition, would give our readers some relief and distress in the middle of our overwhelming macroeconomical information. My workmate wrote reviews on restaurants and I wrote a little column under the title *Here we talk about wines*, signed under the alias *Sommelier*.

I didn't have to wait for the impact of this initiative. After a decade working as a journalist I experienced that an unpretentious column dealing with wine as an object of pleasure and the society's gastronomic culture could have such an echo, this be said proudly, not boastfully. I understood that the wine world —despite this industry's importance— was some sort of microcosm with its own laws and an exacerbated sensitivity not found in other sectors of industry.

I got visitors, letters and phone calls by illustrious representatives of the wine world, others I met in my numerous visits to the Cuyo region, Salta and Río Negro.

That work of investigation and research poured into articles for a considerable number of journals, was taking shape as the *Handbook of Argentine wine* published in 1994 and updated in 2001. It is today presented in this book whose aim is not to revolutionize oenological literature but to make a valuable contribution to those interested in the matter, who may wish to find in a same place a series of information pieces, ideas and advice to get into the wine culture with a greater solvency.

Jorge Dengis

A great challenge

May I proudly introduce myself as Jorge Dengis's faithful assistant since 1993, a year before the first edition, when my uncle Jorge summoned me to the arrangement and organization of the first *Handbook of Argentine wine*. I loved the idea and long months of hard work ushered me into the fascinating world of wine, of where I would never get out. It was a great challenge in an age of quite scanty bibliography, and wine firms found it really novel. The *Handbook* included a page with their principal data, a little history, their products, everything neccesary to get to be known.

It was a real success and by the end of 2001 we produced a little updated version, in spite of our country's entering into an overt economical and political crisis.

From the beginning I learnt to discover the magic found inside a winecup, Jorge was my teacher. I thus perceived the enormous admiration and respect Argentine winemakers he reaped throughout his journalistic career. His greatness, wisdom and values undoubtedly imprinted upon my ethics.

Another person with whom I worked in the *Vinos & Co* magazine was Cristina Córdova, an excellent professional, a journalist specialized in wines and gastronomy, a friend of Jorge's whose transparency, respect and affection also taught me to know this world from the journalistic point of view.

For this new 2006 version we had to face all the changes carried out by wine companies and the ongoing incorporation of new varieties; we focused on solving frequent consumer's doubts and elaborated a guide of accesories for wine service.

I hope you can enter this wonderful world of wine culture where behind each bottle there is a lot of feeling and people await your appraisal.

María Fernanda Dengis

CHAPTER 1

WINE AS EVER

Wine has been accompanying the history of humankind since the most remote times offering a great diversity in taste from different regions, cultures, soil and climate —i.e. terroir— and manufacturing processes.

RJ vineyards.

A ride through History

According to Hugh Johnson — a top expert in this matter, author of the excellent *World Atlas of wines and liquors* translated into many languages— wine history dates back beyond our knowledge.

Wine is believed to have originated in Stone Age, and to be one of the earliest of man's creations. The grape being the only fruit to undergo natural fermentation, once its juice is left inside a vessel the wine will eventually be self-made.

Evidences found by scholars date back to the age of Greek dominance, i.e. one thousand years B.C. We should keep in mind that classic Greeks worshipped a wine god, the revered Dionyssos whose name Roman mythology changed into Bacchus but similarly represented by both: stout, holding a goblet in his hand, forehead garlanded with shiny full-seasoned tendrils. The *Holy Bible* also mentions Noah, a farmer who worked the land and planted a vine, drank its wine and got drunk.

All poets of the days as well as many excerpts from the *Old Testament* dedicate long laudations to wine. We have no doubt that in the famous Dionyssiac or Bacchic feasts wine was appreciated in a quantitative rather than qualitative way; today few doubt that those wines should have been quite deplorable, plain-coloured, sweetish and unmaturated.

Giant wine filter.
Bodega Animaná wine company, Salta.

There's no doubt either that the greatest agricultural event, the most transcendent for wine history, was the introduction of vines into Gaul. When Romans retreated from present-day France in V century, they had laid the foundations of almost all major vineyards of today. According to historical accounts Romans started at Provence, traveled up the Rhône valley reaching Bordeaux, today's undisputed capital of viticulture. There is also proof that there were already vineyards in the Burgundy area by the II century, in Champagne, Moselle and the Rhine by IV century.

In the Middle Age wines were thick, customarily mixed with aromatic herbs, spice, honey and water. Survival of viticulture is owed to monks who popularized the use of wine in religious ceremonies.

With the discovery of bottles and aging in wood by the end of XVII century, quality wine is born, its consumption increased from demand by the higher classes.

Viniculture's thrust to its present state started in XIX century but it should be kept in mind that in that century the terrible Phylloxera plague almost finished all vineyards in major European

Wooden wine presses. Bodega Carmelo Patti, Mendoza.

countries. In those dreadful years Latin America was the life raft for Old World vineyards when expert agronomists discovered that scions grafted onto roots of vines from this area withstood the predatory pest. In that period this industry fell into a deep depression, thriving only the producers from unaffected areas. Activity started to recover in XX century but World War I resulted in a modification in habits, consumption of table wine increased as a result.

The viticultural map has been broadening since a few decades ago, with important areas being increasingly incorporated such as Napa and Sonoma valley in northern California, South Africa, Australia, New Zealand, Algeria and former Soviet Union with quite promising perspectives.

XIX-century pump. Bodega Carmelo Patti, Mendoza.

Old epoxy tank used to preserve oak-wood casks. Bodega Carmelo Patti, Mendoza.

All these new areas as well as the already existing ones which kept expanding, are ecologically fit for this crop. As the same varieties are not grown in every area, wines coming from each are considerably differentiated in colour, aroma and taste.

History is of course far from coming to an end these days because technology, in crop as well as manufacturing, is in constant progress and areas of the globe, some time ago deemed inviable, will be predictably incorporated into viticulture.

The making of wine

For wine manufacturing, the first to take into account is the *terroir* or home place which encompasses weather, temperature, soil, insulation time and water received by vines.

In the Southern Hemisphere grape harvest takes place between the first week of February and the first days of April. Harvest is carried out with machinery, sometimes manually in 20 kg baskets. It's usually done very early in the morning or by night in order to prevent heat from starting an undesired fermentation process.

Grinding is the following step as bunches reach the press. They are conveyed into a machine that clears the woody structure away from the grapes. The following step is pressing of grapes for their juice. Virgin juice or *must* is then pumped into fermentation pools or vats (along with pulp, peel and seed).

Today's presses are quite sophisticated to prevent traumatic disruption of grapes. Rubber balloons or bags are used which, as they inflate, gently squeeze grapes against perforated cylinders, must flowing through holes into pipes from where it is pumped to pools and vats. All the process is carried out in an inert atmosphere, another resource to prevent oxygen from permeating into the elaboration.

Stainless-steel tanks and wooden casks. Bodega Finca Sophenia, Mendoza.

What it takes to turn the grape into wine is fermentation, a simple, absolutely natural process. It's a chemical phenomenon where grape sugar is transformed into alcohol and carbon dioxide. Yeasts — microorganisms living in grape peel— are its agents. Peel-breaking is enough for them to start working the sugar that constitutes 30% of pulp, thus starting fermentation, that is transformation of *must* (virgin juice) into wine.

In normal conditions yeast would act until all the sugar in the must turned into alcohol or the alcohol level in wine reached roughly 15% of volume. On the rare occasions when grapes are very sweet yeast action stops here, thus halting fermentation.

This process is carried out in big pools or tanks which may be made of stainless steel or mortar lined inside with epoxy resins that give the walls a glassy appearance.

After this step vinification proceeds differently for white or red wines.

Red wine vinification

Fermentation is carried out by natural yeasts in grape peel and those selected, thus starting consumption of sugar in must and its conversion into ethyl alcohol and carbon dioxide. This way is formed the famous "boiling" must called *tumultuous*.

Between the fifth and eighth day the first stage is finished. A temperature between 25 °C and 30 °C [77-86 °F] is kept so fermentation slows down until all of natural sugar is consumed, thus ending this step.

Different stages then follow: maceration achieved by contact between must and marc where all natural pigments, tannins and aromatic compounds are present. All these components are transferred to the must, adding to the future wine's personality: colour, body and aroma. This stage can last for hours according to the quality of wine desired. The enologist sets the endpoint, when solid natural sediment is separated from liquid.

Here starts the work of cleansing dead yeast deposited in the vat's bottom after settling, to achieve stable clarity and colour; of clarifying, filtering and centrifugating.

Then comes the time for rest called aging; it may happen in tanks or casks made of oak wood (French or American). According to the type of finished product desired, duration will vary between three and twenty-four months.

Once the desired wine is obtained it is bottled, where it settles down and acquires its optimum maturity point. This is done in an inert atmosphere to protect it from oxygen.

The chemical process inside the bottle is a reduction, which amounts to a loss of oxygen that permeates outward through a cork still uncovered by its lead or plastic capsule. This deoxygenation process is the reason behind the recommendation of opening red wines some time before drinking, so that they can "breathe" thus acquiring their full personality.

Wooden casks.
Bodega Terrazas de los Andes, Mendoza.

Description of several red wines

FEATURE	CHARACTERISTICS
Colour intensity	Colourless, pale, medium, intense, deep
Hue	Violaceous, purple, cherry, garnet, ruby, tile, chestnut/reddish mahogany
Transparency	Bright, dull, turbid
Development	Young, evolved, very evolved, old

AROMA -BOUQUET	CHARACTERISTICS
State	Clean, contaminated (sulfurous, vinegar-like, mouldy, etc.)
Flowery	Violet, rose
Fruity	Berries: cassis, blackberry, currant, strawberry
	Pit fruits: plum, cherry, sour cherry
	Seed fruits: grape, pear, apple
	Dry: almond, filbert, walnut, dried plum, fig
Botanical	Fresh-mowed grass, mint, eucalyptus
	Fresh: green peppers, olive
	Dry: tea, tobacco
Woody	Phenolic: vanilla
	Resiny: cedar, oak
	Toasted: smoke, coffee
Spicy	Black pepper, clove, cinnamon
Caramel	Molasses, chocolate, soybean sauce
Microbiological	Yeast, lactic
Bouquet	Oxidation, reduction

PALATE	CHARACTERISTICS
Sweetness	Dry, demi-sec, sweet (mild)
Acidity	Acidulous (poor acidity), refreshing, acid
Bitterness	Non-bitter, slightly, medium, notoriously bitter
Flavour/ intensity	Weak, medium, intense
	Fruity, winy
Body	Light, medium, complex, heavy
Finishing	Short of mouth, medium, long, velvety

HARMONY	CHARACTERISTICS
Development	Undeveloped, mature, very mature
Equilibrium	Balanced, unbalanced

White wine vinification

This vinification is more careful than the preceding, starting at the harvest. Maceration should not be prolonged because if marc stays too long with the must it will transfer tannins and pigments into the wine in the making.

Solid substances are first decanted to the tank's bottom to achieve a translucent appearance; clarification is then carried out by adding natural elements such as egg white to speed up precipitation.

Fermentation is the following step, slower for white wines in order to preserve wine aromas. It takes place at a very low temperature (between 15 °C and 20 °C [59-68 °F]) using powerful refrigerating equipment to slow down the process to render it more controllable and prevent any oxidation, i.e. oxygen intake. It is then transferred into steel tanks where fermentation lasts between 10 and 20 days, colour turning very intense yellow.

Whites do not undergo a secondary fermentation known as "malolactic", with the exception of *Chardonnay* fermented in oak casks for better complexity.

Regarding preservation, white wines are aged for shorter time to ensure their fineness. Once bottled they are ready for the marketplace.

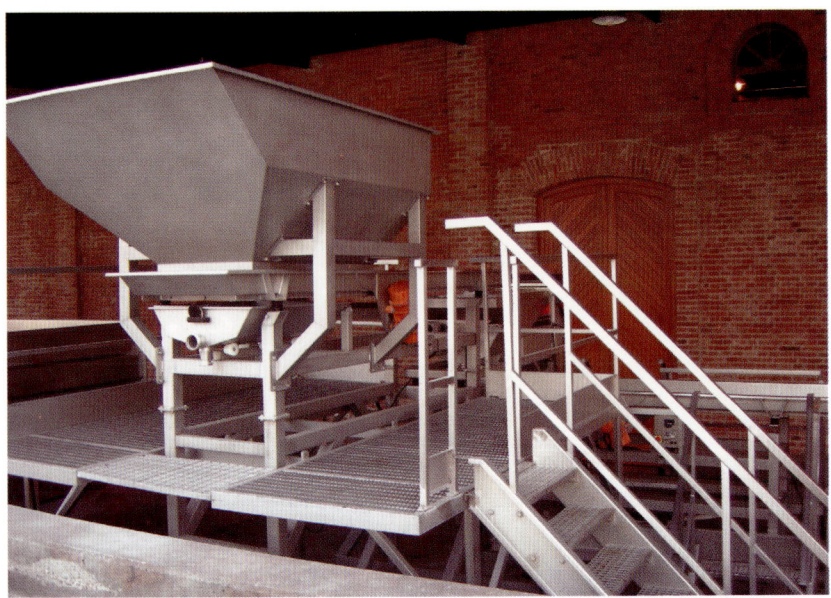

Wine press. Bodega Terrazas de los Andes, Perdriel, Mendoza.

Description of white wines

FEATURE	CHARACTERISTICS
Colour intensity	Pale, medium, intense
Hue	Greenish/yellow, yellow, straw, golden, yellow, gold, amber, ocher
Transparency	Bright, dull, turbid
Development	Young, scarcely evolved, evolved, very evolved, old

AROMA-BOUQUET	CHARACTERISTICS
State	Clean, contaminated (sulfurous, vinegar-like, mouldy, etc.)
Flowery	Linalol, geranium, violet, jasmine, orange, rose
Fruity	Tropical: pineapple, banana, melon
	Citric: lemon, grapefruit
	Pit fruits: peach, apricot
	Seed fruits: grape, pear, apple
	Nut: almond, filbert, walnut
Botanical	Fresh-mowed lawn, mint, eucalyptus
Woody	Phenolic: vanilla
	Resiny: cedar, oak
	Toasted: smoky
Caramel	Honey, butter
Microbiological	Yeast, lactic
Bouquet	Oxidation, reduction

PALATE	CHARACTERISTICS
Sweetness	Dry, demi-sec, sweet (mild)
Acidity	Acidulous (poor acidity), refreshing, acid
Bitterness	Non-bitter, slightly, medium, notoriously bitter
Flavour/ intensity	Weak, medium, intense
	Fruity, winy
Body	Light, medium, complex, heavy
Finishing	Short of mouth, medium, long, velvety

HARMONY	CHARACTERISTICS
Development	Undeveloped, mature, very mature
Equilibrium	Balanced, unbalanced

Chapter 2

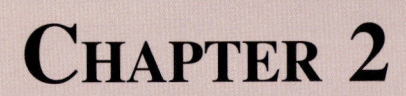

Argentina, a wine-bearing country

*A*rgentine vineyards grow between 22° S and 42° S more than 2,400 km [1,490 mi.] along the Andean piedmont between the provinces of Salta and Río Negro, with a diversity of climate and soil that makes every region a unique terroir *for high-quality wines.*

Terrazas de los Andes vineyards.

A history of wine in Argentina

History of Argentine viticulture dates back to early European settlement, since cultivation of wine was closely linked to Spanish colonists' agricultural practices. Conquistadors are sad to have carried to Cuzco (Peru) by mid-XVI century the first grapevines of the species *Vitis vinifera*, ideal for wine-making. They were then carried to Chile in 1551, then introduced into present-day Argentina.

Many believe the first vineyards to have been planted in the province of Santiago del Estero in 1554 by Mercedary priest Juan Cidrón. According to this theory father Cidrón and Juan Jufré —the second founder of Mendoza city— implanted the first vineyards in today's top-producing Argentine province. Juan Jufré was a warrior-cum-farmer and his teachings are likely to be the foundation stone of viticultural activity in the provinces of Mendoza and San Juan.

Some disagree thinking Conquistadors to have brought the first grapevines. Their hypothesis is based upon the fact that a few years after the foundation of Mendoza, the friar Reginaldo Lizárraga writes that the province boasted a notable progress in wine-making by supplying other regions.

Land brokerage started by 1700, farms quoted according to their number of vineyards and their closeness to the main square first in Mendoza, later in San Juan, La Rioja and Salta.

Top: old oak casks.
Left: watering of a vineyard.
Bodega Terrazas de los Andes, Mendoza.

Argentine wine

Argentina has *terroirs* that produce wines with their own personality. With more than 200,000 hectares [494,210 acres] planted with vineyards it's the fifth wine producer and the sixth consumer worldwide. There is an undisputed preference to red varieties, especially *Cabernet sauvignon* and *Malbec*.

Its geography circumscribed to the 22° S - 42° S; 2,400 km strip along the foot of the Andes. It yields an average 100 hundredweight per hectare [4,460 tons/acre].

Deep, permeable, organic-matter poor soils favour the development of this culture.

Argentina's viticulture is undergoing a very important turn. Great investors, domestic and foreign, have totally or partially bought wine-producing companies and lands.

Renowned enologists such as Michel Rolland and Paul Hobbs permanently advise several producers in Mendoza and Salta.

Planted surface in each province (in hectares & *acres*)

Mendoza	San Juan	La Rioja	Río Negro	Catamarca	Salta	Neuquén	Other
140,114.7	39,877.0	7,460.2	5,336.1	1,817.5	796.9	75.2	656.2
346,231	*98,538.2*	*18434.5*	*13,185.8*	*4,491.1*	*1,969.2*	*185.8*	*1,621.5*

Source: INV's database on Argentine Wine Producers.

J&F Lurton vineyard, Mendoza.

Argentine wine-bearing regions

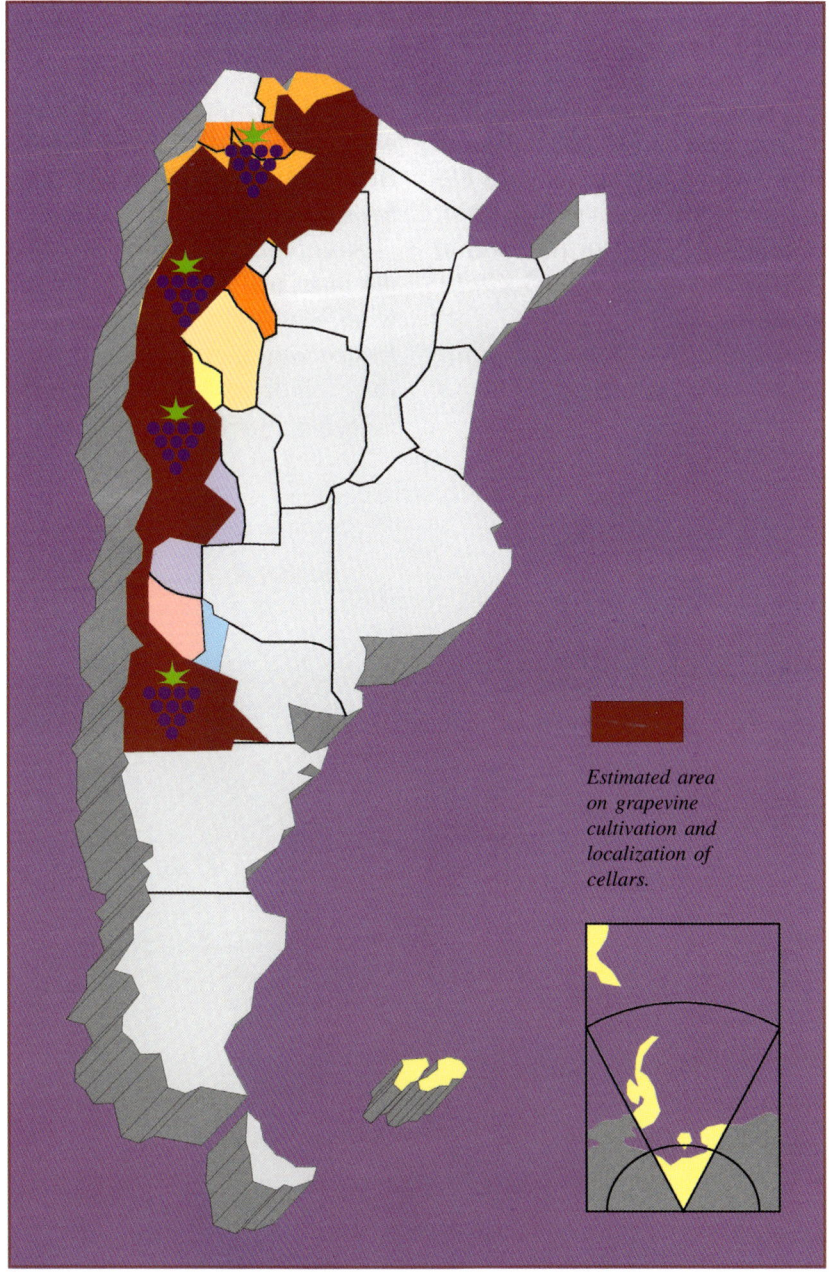

Estimated area on grapevine cultivation and localization of cellars.

Exporting Argentina

Exports of wine and must 2005 reached 33,815.460 dollars in June, which represents a 25.8% increase with respect to June 2004.

Overseas sales in this period reached a volume of 155,129.61 hectoliters [4,098,091 gal] representing a 4.89% increase, net revenues amounting to 23.73 million dollars.

The target market of sparkling wine sales were the markets of Brazil, the United Kingdom, Peru, Sweden and the Netherlands.

According to the INV, in 2004 the main purchasers of Argentine wine were the United States, the United Kingdom, Brazil, Canada, the Netherlands, Denmark, Paraguay, Russia and Germany.

Of the total volume of wine exported Mendoza sold 212 million dollars and San Juan 7.5 million.

The Mendoza province was incorporated as the eight member of the selected international group *Great Wine Capital* (GWC) from its integral involvement in the process of growing, manufacturing and distributing wines with certified identification, thus bringing commercial and touristic profits.

The GWC network was created in 1998 by winemakers from Bordeaux (France), Melbourne (Australia), San Francisco and Napa Valley (U.S.A.), Florence (Italy), Porto (Portugal), later joined by representatives from Rioja and Bilbao (Spain) and Cape Town (South Africa).

Terrazas de los Andes vineyard, Mendoza.

Wine-bearing regions

Argentina is ranked as worldwide fifth producer of wine, belonging to New World wine-producing countries (Australia, U.S.A., South Africa, Argentina and Chile). Two distinctive characteristics of our wines are the different terroirs and combinations of climate, soil and variety. Vineyards grow with the Andes' imposing background ensuring appropriate conditions for their development: from irrigation with melting ice and scarce precipitation, to a considerable night/day temperature range enabling development of aroma and colour.

It's necessary to travel every region to discover its distinct expression as a wine.

Three important planted regions can be distinguished in our country: Northern Zone, Central Zone and Southern Zone.

Luigi Bosca vineyards, Mendoza.

Domingo Hnos. vineyards, Salta.

Implantation zones in Argentina

Northern Zone

Salta

The country's northernmost wine-producing region.

The Calchaquí Valleys are found here at a 1,500 m [*4,920 ft*] height above sea level.

Ideal weather, soil, height and humidity add up for a natural acidity this is why this region is matchless worldwide for production of *Torrontés* (the principal variety).

Other varieties are *Malbec, Cabernet sauvignon* and to a lesser extent *Syrah, Chardonnay* and *Tannat*.

Major companies are located in: Cafayate (25° S); Tacuil, Colomé, Molinos, San Carlos, Animaná and San Pedro de Yacochuya.

La Rioja

In the Denomination of Origin "Valles de Famatina-Torrontés Riojano" (Chilecito department) fine and sparkling wines of the *Torrontés* variety are produced.

Vineyards are located between 900 and 1,400 m [*2,950 - 4,590 ft*] above sea level, with a remarkable incidence on the quality of its wines.

Wines are being produced with the *Syrah* and *Chardonnay* varieties with excellent results.

Catamarca

A desertic climate that needs drop-by-drop irrigation.

A broad temperature range favours production of high-quality wines with red varieties such as *Syrah, Bonarda, Cabernet sauvignon* and the white variety *Torrontés*.

Wine producers are found between Tinogasta and Fiambalá (all the Catamarca Valley region, close to the Chilean border).

Its main feature are olive groves and production of high-quality olive oil for export.

Central Zone

Mendoza

The top zone for the quality and quantity of wines it produces.

The Andes has its highest peaks here, a major factor on climate influence.

Dry hot summer and short, cold winter with scanty precipitation. Dry climate with rivers of strong currents. Wide temperature range favours balanced ripening of grapes.

Two producing regions: the Mendoza river catchment and San Rafael to the South.

The Northern sector is in its turn subdivided into four areas: North, East, Upper Mendoza River and Uco Valley. Near Mendoza city the localities of Luján de Cuyo and Maipú are found, the home of the most traditional companies.

In the Southern sector vineyards are irrigated by Atuel and Diamante rivers.

70% of the country's vinicultural production is concentrated in this region.

San Juan

Next in importance to Mendoza in implanted area and vinicultural production.

Major productive areas are located in the valleys of Tulum, El Zonda and Ullum, located to the West of the capital city.

In the last few years, the Pedernal area microclimate, in the South East, allowed the setllement of varietal cellars.

Once characterized by the production of ordinary wines, in modern times these were modified from the very *terroir* to technical resources by young entrepreneurs committed to the quality of their vineyards

A dry hot region with scarcely exploited land, artificial irrigation and absence of hailstorms -features that guarantee quite interesting wines.

South Zone

Río Negro

The world's southernmost wine-bearing region, with vineyards between 37° S and 40° S.

The climate is dry and continental, the Summer with hot days and very cold nights, with scant rains that make artificial irrigation necessary.

The principal hazard to vineyard is frost, which can modify grape ripening.

The productive area is located between Limay and Neuquén rivers, called Río Negro Upper Valley; Mid Valley and East Colorado river.

Merlot and *Pinot noir* varieties find the right *terroir* as well as *Sauvignon blanc*, *Sémillon* and *Chardonnay*, differentiated from other produced in other regions.

Neuquén

Productive area: Neuquén river Valley in San Patricio del Chañar, in the Añelo department.

Arid climate, scant rains and strong winds. Early or late frost restricts cultivation of varieties with a long vegetative cycle.

Companies have an adequate infrastructure for tourist hosting, wine tasting and restaurants with privileged views.

The most used varieties in Argentina

Our country's wine-making is now some centuries old, the first grapevine scions planted by the Jesuits by 1557 but it was just in the last quarter of XIX century when professional wine-making started. There are many centenarian companies; the origin of the vast majority, however, is nearer in time.

Argentine viticulture was started by immigrants arriving at the country by late XIX century, Italian in the first place; secondly Spanish and German. Oddly enough, French contribution took some time to come but it is very important today, if not from the number of companies, from their quality standards and enological know-how, their contact with modern technology and marketing experience.

In spite of the major Italian contribution, varieties brought by them were mostly of French origin, perhaps because early XIX century well-to-do Argentines consumed French wines.

We shall list below the most abundant and frequent varieties in Argentina. The list is not exhaustive but enumerative. We should keep in mind that there are over five thousand grape varieties in the world, less than one hundred fit for wine-making.

White varieties

Chardonnay: highest-ranked among its congeners. Used to produce the finest white varieties, it is frequently the foundation of some generic white wines and the most relevant domestic champagne. It produces rich, balanced wines with good aroma and taste as well as remarkable persistence. Its aromas are described by fresh butter, filberts, toasted bread, apple, melon, peach, etc.
Found in the Maipú zone, Tupungato and San Rafael in Mendoza; also grown with excellent results in the Río Negro Upper Valley. This variety is used under the universally renowned denomination of origin *Chablis*.

Chardonay grapes, Terrazas de los Andes.

Chenin: the most extensively grown fine white variety. Mistaken for years with *Pinot blanc*, the error was opportunely corrected by the National Institute of Agropecuary Technology (INTA). This Agency developed a colossal ampelographic work (*ampelography*: scientific discipline studying grape varieties). In Argentina this variety achieves very good quality— pale, elegant, singularly fine wines are obtained from it. Its aroma is dominated by peach. It is some experts' opinion that *Chenin* and *Pinot de la Loire* are two denominations for a same variety. According to others they are two like-looking sisters, not identical twins.
Most frequently found in the San Rafael area (Mendoza).

Sauvignon* or *Sauvignon blanc: the second finest variety after *Chardonnay*. It's preferred to harvest it not too ripe in order to preserve its acidity, which gives it a particular dryness. Blended with *Sémillon* in France it produces the best white wines of Bordeaux.
Its wines have botanical and smoky flavours; perfumes of cassis, valerian, and flint sparkle are also detected.

Sémillon: long underrated in Argentina from the low-quality wines produced under its name, these undoubtedly corresponded to some other variety or very badly manufactured. Nowadays, however, it is renowned for the high quality of the wines produced with it. A singular plenitude is achieved by wines made of *Sémillon* in Río Negro and the Tupungato area in Mendoza.
Its wines are dry, with body and aroma described by lemon, acacia, linden, vervain and avocado.

Riesling: a conflictive variety in Argentina, the origin of implanted vineyards is yet unknown, i.e. whether from the Rhine (Alsace) or the Friulan tokai (= tokay) of Italian origin, not Hungarian. Wines made of the authentic *Riesling* have an unmistakable aroma and show a soft natural sweetness that renders them quite elegant.

Traminer: this variety comes from Alsace where two types are grown which are like first cousins: *Traminer* proper and *Gewürztraminer* with its trademark spicy flavour. There is little production in Argentina. It gives a perfumed wine, poorly acid with fruity aromas.

***Torrontés*:** perhaps the most distinctive variety of Argentine wine —including both red and white wines— beacause Argentina it is practically the only country to produce it. It has been called the "Maradona" or "Gardel" of grapes in the wine world because Argentina is worldwide identified through it. There are two basic types: *Riojana* and *Mendocina*, however, according to some experts there is a third type, the *Sanjuanina*. The *Riojana* is the most representative and the *Torrontés* from Cafayate (Salta) are made of it. Wines produced from this variety have reaped many international awards. Its flavour, quite different from other whites, has captivated tasters from many countries as aromatic, with a slightly bitter aftertaste.

***Ugni blanc*:** used in many white blends, it is a part of the *coupage* of many wines (the foundation of Champagne making). Known as *Trebiona* in Italy, as *Saint Emilion blanc* in France. Used in Champagne to naturally increase the degree of acidity.

***Pedro Ximénez*:** according to the INTA the vineyards grown in Argentina under that name are not like the one produced in other countries under the same name. Seldom used alone, in our country there is an excellent foundation for wines denominated *jerez* (sherry) or *manzanilla*.

***Viognier*:** a semi-classic variety grown in the northern Rhône area in France. Its wine is spicy with a hint of moscatel grapes and violet.

Terrazas de los Andes.

Red varieties

Cabernet sauvignon: just like *Chardonnay* among whites, this one is "the Queen" of red varieties. Alone or in company it participates in most top-rated fine Argentine wines. A tough variety, a little wary and wild, by no means easily tamed. Its *bouquet* enhanced by aging which also dampens its natural astringency, determined by its high content of tannins. It requires careful elaboration but the results obtained justify such dedication. In France this variety produced the best red wines under the denomination of origin *Medoc*. Good results are also frequently obtained with it in California, Chile and Australia.

Cabernet sauvignon grapes, Terrazas de los Andes.

As a young wine it is characterized by its hardness, with marked acidity and present harsh tannins; once it maturated it is deep, fleshy and complex, ideally mated with our traditional *asado*. Its most distinctive flavour is pepper and red fruit.

Merlot: a distinguished variety, genetically related to *Cabernet sauvignon* with which "mates" quite fine giving it a fruity flavour, elegance and roundness. It produces varietals of remarkable fineness and personality, less acid and more fruity. A subtle variety but with by no means a negligible body.
Grown in the Upper Mendoza river and San Rafael, another privileged area being Río Negro Upper Valley.

Malbec: the most extensively grown and characteristic of our red varieties. In Argentina *Malbec* (or *Malbeck*, as there is no consensus about its correct spelling) offers really exceptional qualities, especially in the Maipú department, particularly the localities of Cruz de Piedra, Luján de Cuyo and Vistalba (Mendoza). It could well be called the "battle steed" of countless Argentine wines, formerly also employed in table wines. Back then it hadn't been realized yet that it can give wines of superior quality when well worked. Today, many producers have discovered its virtues, obtaining wines that won important prizes in international contests. It is many experts' opinion that *Malbec* achieves a better quality in our country than in its original homeland, France. This is also acknowledged by the French, a point not worth ignoring when we take into account their exacerbated patriotic pride. Its wine has a good body and rustic palate.

Malbec grapes, Terrazas de los Andes.

Pinot noir: the variety with which the best wines of Burgundy are produced. In Argentina its cultivation is growing (until recently only a relatively small area was planted with it). Argentine tasters and *connoîsseurs* are learning to appraise this variety, which can produce wines of singular quality, yet more difficult to accept in a first encounter from their subtlety and rich spectrum of elegant flavours. Experts recommend uncorking wines made of this variety quite long —even up to 24 hours before— in advance to their consumption so they can oxygenate and fully acquire their particular palate.

Syrah: also known as *Sirah* or *Petit Sirah*. Thought to come from the Shiraz area in ancient Persia (hence the evolution of its name), from where it was carried to France by Crusaders. It now constitutes there the foundation for wines of the Côtes du Rhone area and the famous *Châteauneuf-du Pape*, perhaps the most renowned outside Bordeaux and Burgundy regions. In Argentina many produces started producing it as a varietal with quite flattering results. Some time ago it was mistaken for Italian *Balsamina*, with which it is related to some extent. It produces a sumptuous, velvety wine with a long aftertaste.

Syrah grapes, Terrazas de los Andes.

Barbera d'Asti: a variety also long mistaken with *Bonarda*, which doesn't achieve its level of quality. Originary from the Piedmont region in Italy. In Argentina grown near San Rafael south of Mendoza, a good wine area. Good colour and body but poor in elegance. More often used in blends.

Lambrusco: according to INTA the variety known under this name in Argentina (which in Italy gives fruity, slightly *frizzante* wines) is in fact the less-quality *Refosco*. It produces strongly-coloured wines but with mediocre taste. Improving colour is just its role in blends.

Sangiovese: a typically Italian variety, it is the origin of most famous *Chianti*. It does very well in Argentina. Once mistaken for *Lambrusco*, an error corrected by the INTA.
Young, soft wines are produced with this variety, but intensely red coloured and strongly fruity.

Tempranillo: native to Spain, it managed to find interest from producers and consumers in Argentina. Its wines have a certain tannic character, with good structure and remarkable density.

Bonarda: a rough grape very popular in Argentina, it is from Piedmont in Italy. Generally wines made of it are not expensive because of its high yield; however, with appropriate care it is possible to obtain good must for quality wine.
Its wines have an intense violaceous hue and high aromatic presence.

Back from harvesting work. J&F Lurton wine company.

Generic or blend wines

Since a while ago the name "generic" has been given to wines obtained from two ore more different varieties, opposed to "varietals" produced from only one variety.

As a matter of semantic correctness I prefer calling non-varietals "blend" wines, since according to the dictionary the term *genus* (in the root of "genre", "gender" and "generic") designates a set of objects similar to each other from possessing one or more essentially common characters. Logic also teaches "genus" to have a greater extension than "species". From the above, if grapevine varieties are considered species, their genus should be a mother grape encompassing them all. The only element fitting this category is *Vitis vinifera*, i.e. the type of grape right for wine-making. To summarize, it's this author's opinion that the sum of two or more blends does not make a wine "generic". In other words, the sum of some species does not constitute a genus since this should by definition comprise them all.

Now let's get over the *Oxford English Dictionary* and leave the follow-up of this polemic to those with a special interest. What can be said is that before the rise of varietal wines, those produced by a blend of two or more varieties —typical of the Bordeaux region in France— were never labeled 'generic' but simply fine red or white. In some counted cases, the rear label informed the varieties used in the blend (never the proportions). In others, just the drinker's savvy was to establish the identity of varieties in the *coupage* (a French expression designating the content of a bottle of "generic" or "blend" wine). Some are plain (*Cabernet-Merlot* or *Chardonnay-Chenin*), other singularly complicated. Some *Châteauneuf-du-Pape*, typical of the Rhône area in southern France resulted from the combination of over a dozen different varieties.

Many Argentine companies are intransigently partisan of this way of making wine, for instance, Bodegas y Viñedos López. None of its wines (Rincón Famoso, Châteauvieux or Château Montchenot) is a varietal. All of them result from an expert blend jealously kept secret, locked up just like in the fairy tales of our childhood. The exception is the white Selección blanco: a 100% *Sémillon* varietal.

The blend of two or more varieties has never resulted from the winemaker's fancy. On the other hand, it's a custom whose origins are lost in the mists of History, though its goal has always been the obtention of better products. The undisputed "queen" of red varieties *Cabernet sauvignon* is no easy wine. When fresh it is aggressive, very tannic, and such traits reflect as a notorious astringency well-perceived by our gums. In order to smooth such edges in Bordeaux *Cabernet sauvignon* is blended with *Merlot*, a variety, equivalent to its little sister, yet very much softer and more elegant. Our old acquaintance the *Malbec*, is also used to render it more winy and give it a rounder palate. Precisely, the art of *blend* or *coupage* consists of finding the exact proportion of every variety to achieve a balanced product; sumnarizing, better than the sum of its components. A centenarian art, that which achieves its height after the XIX century just in the Bordeaux region.

Of course, blending of wine—red or white—is not exclusively French but also practiced in Italy, Spain and obviously in Argentina, which traditionally followed. European habits and mores. Great wines in History, from the classical Mouton-Rothschild or Château Lafitte, as well as the foundations for the best champagnes result from a blend of diverse varieties.

In all cases or at least most frequently, there is a predominant variety accounting for 40 to 50% of finished wine. The ones blended into the principal variety give it new virtues, or soften or round its nature.

The aim of the above reflections is to warn the insufficiently informed reader about the basic incorrectness of the assertion that generic wines are superior to varietals, or the converse. Everything is inherently subjective when it comes to palate since it is up to our senses, different in each human being, to determine preferences. While some choose dense, strong-bodied, overwhelmingly aggressive wines other prefer the soft, simple, little-structured, easy-to-drink wines.

Varietal wines and the Californian "revolution"

In the early 1970s some producers from Argentina started watching with growing interest what was happening in northern California (U.S.A.), a region where a silent yet persistent technological revolution had been developing in the wine-making industry, traditionally attached to craftwork (the main wine-bearing areas being Napa and Sonoma valleys near San Francisco).

Beyond technology, what was beginning to prevail was a "vinicultural philosophy", which while not too distant in the fundamental from what had been traditionally done in the rest of the world made some clear and conclusive statements that can be summarized as follows:

• Varieties very well selected in the regions of origin, principally France but also Italy, Spain and Germany. Imported scions started to be profusely planted to the point of covering over 200,000 hectares today— a very similar figure to that registered in Argentina, having an older viticultural tradition than California.

• Ecologically right soils, well-drained, located in areas with a rather scarce average annual rain. What the sky won't give is supplied by rather sophisticated irrigation systems.

- Harvest at the time of optimal ripening of grapes.

- Extremely careful collection of bunches to avoid deterioration of grapes which must arrive at the press in the best possible condition.

- Fermentation at very low temperatures for white wines to prevent it from being tumultuous, which results in the loss of most good qualities contributed by the right varieties.

- Little or no wood for red wines. When matured in wood they won't spend longer than six months in 225 liters [53.44 gal] casks of fresh oak.

- Last but not least among the Californian techniques was making wines of a single variety of grape, hence the name "varietal". In some cases a variety predominates—75 to 80% of the total —completing the rest with other varieties allowing for improvement— or "rounding" the palate of the final product. Most Californian varietals, however, are 100% of a single variety.

Wines thus obtained are fruity, balanced, with a well-defined palate.

The boom of varietal wine, which started in California but then spread to all the world's important viticultural regions eventually became a sort of variety *apartheid*, where they seemingly aspire to avoid mingling with their congeners.

California's top varietals come from the two varieties thought to have the highest pedigree: the red *Cabernet sauvignon* and the white *Chardonnay*. However, the most extended varietal is made from a variety unknown in Argentina—namely *Zinfandel*, which can be said to fill the U.S. niche equivalent to that of our *Malbec*.

Grown in extensive areas, this variety has a yield well over that of the two above mentioned. So much for the commonalities between *Zinfandel* and *Malbec*: their flavours are by no means similar. Both are personal, pleasant and full, but completely different from each other.

As pointed above that enological revolution prompted several producers to visit California, see the premises of companies that produced varietals, talk with enologists, consult technicians at UC Davis—majoring in enology—and import that philosophy along with the machinery for its implementation.

A historical pioneer for this kind of wines in our country was Bodegas San Telmo which after ten years (selection of imported stock, implantation, building of premises, incorporation of machinery, maturing of vineyards and production of the first harvests) in 1983 launched three varietals: *Cabernet sauvignon*, *Malbec* and *Chenin*. It later incorporated a *Chardonnay* and a *Merlot*. Their success was quite flattering since these wines have a very well-defined personality with marked flavour appreciated by a considerable segment of consumers. In some way they resemble 1950s or 1960s Argentine wines characterized by their rich presence and body.

Then came Bodegas Martins, a well-known name in the wine-making family from Mr. Rui Martins, a Portuguese immigrant and a manufacturer as well as supplier of high-quality cork. From the beginning his company was managed by his son, Juan José "Tito" Martins. Right from the start they gambled high by simultaneously launching six varietals with an excellent price/quality ratio: three red—*Cabernet sauvignon*, *Malbec* y *Merlot*—and three white —*Chardonnay*, *Sauvignon blanc* y *Chenin*.

Almost simultaneously a new producer was riding the varietal wave: Leoncio Arizu with his brand "Luigi Bosca" which took a different path for market penetration. Company manager Alberto Arizu, a renowned agronomist, lived up to the principle "the wine is born in the vineyard" by carrying out a thorough work with his own aimed at organic wines, i.e. vineyards free from synthetic fertilizers or pesticides. Today his line, quite depurated in quality and presentation, musters a great variety of wines.

Currently all companies have lines with very good varietal and bivarietal wines, though not all follow the Californian manufacturing process.

Chapter 3

WINE TASTING

Sampling of wine is an art with elements of science as well as cumulative knowledge based on experience. Wine is a result of culture and an object of pleasure that needs to be interpreted through our senses.

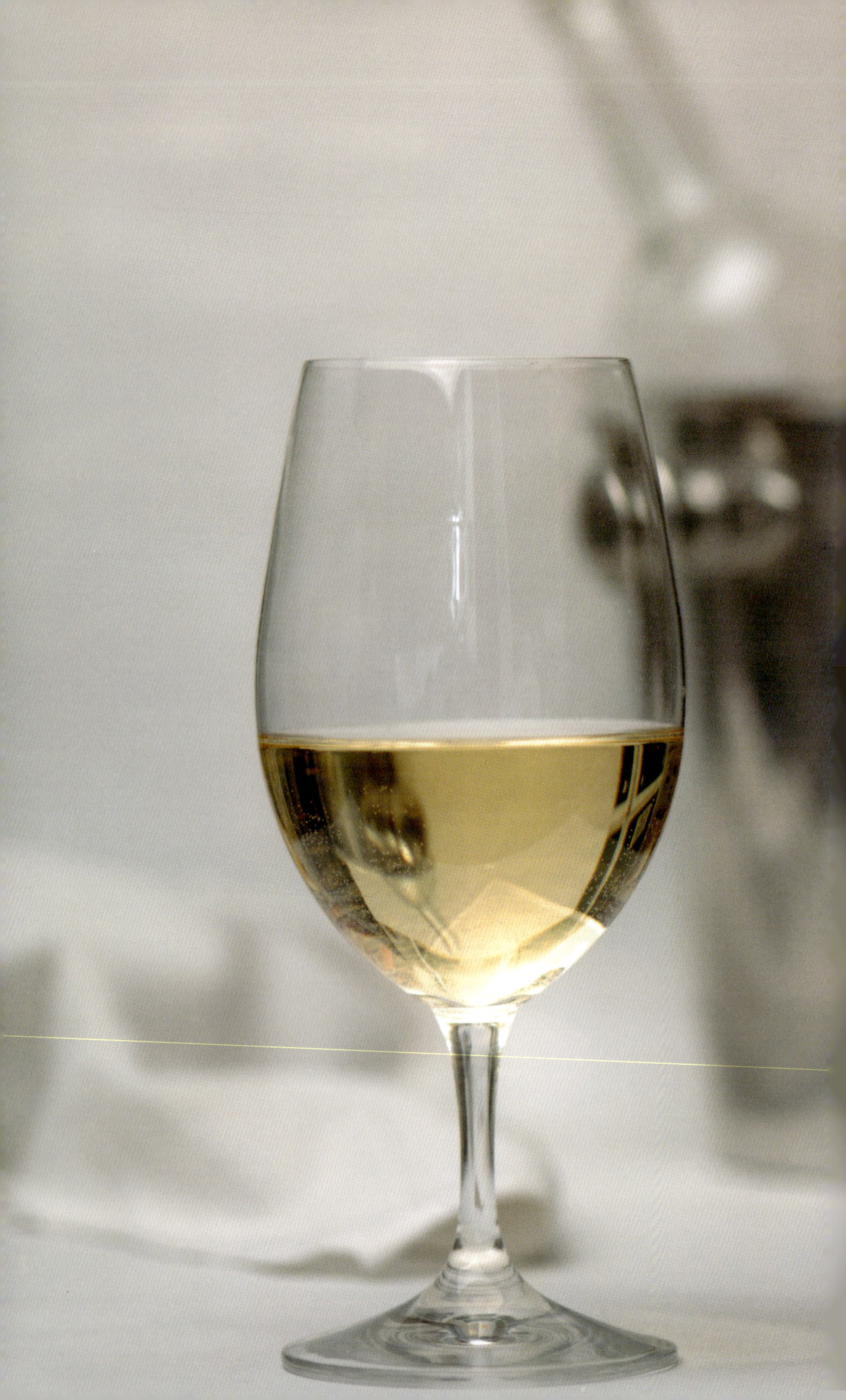

Sampling: a game for training wine-tasters

As expressed in other chapters this *Handbook* is dedicated to those in the process of initiation into the knowledge of wine, whatever their motivation: be it sheer love for the beverage, a personal aim to broaden their cultural horizon or acquire an asset for social performance. Neither will its reading entail the reader's instantly becoming a scholar as this calls for a lifetime of dedication.

International experts, i.e. those who participate in contests celebrated in different locations all over the world are not necessarily enologists but *connoîsseurs* in the broadest sense of the term, having earned their place by their merits. The reader probably ignores to what extent it is possible to know this matter so full of subtlety.

To start discovering our own palate let's lay the foundations of what could be called a *household blind- sampling game,* meant not to make us international experts but as an entertainment to share with our friends.

To make our sampling game interesting several players will participate in, no less than four, up to half a dozen.

Wine bar, Bodega Ruca Malén wine company.

Household blind-sampling game

What it takes

• Four bottles of wine of a same variety (they can be selected from different price levels to ensure comparability). Open them a while before starting the game so that the wine can breathe by removing both cork and capsule. Disguise the bottles efficiently to prevent identification by participants, e.g. by wrapping them in a napkin or thick paper. Then number bottles 1 to 4.

• Wine-cups.

• Paper and pencil.

The game

1. Every participant is given a sheet of paper to take notes.

2. The game conductor (e.g. who purchased the bottles) serves every participant no more than one third of a goblet.

3. Participants must individually judge the beverage's classical four features: appearance, aroma, palate and harmony (See wine descriptive tables in *Chapter 1*). Each of these shall be rated 1 to 5 to avoid excessive complexity, i.e. any sample's maximum possible score will be 20.

4. As a round is finished and wine rated by all participants the game's climax comes, what could be called bottle *strip-tease*.

Of course, in this case the purpose of blind tasting is not to identify the wine tasted but to express our opinion on each sample. Some surprises usually come as the bottles' disguises are removed. Scores diverge because of two factors: for one it's a matter of personal opinion, hence it varies from one person to another; for other, there are customary easy graders and mean appraisers.

Another quite frequent surprise is the realization that best scores not always go to the most expensive wines. This is why bottle-masking is indispensable: nobody is immune to the conditioning exerted by a renowned brand.

This sampling game we propose is an imitation of blind tasting practiced in great international contests; our reason to recommend it is that you can learn from it, it's attractive and players have a good time because nobody losses since all players may drink good wine.

Needless to say, the game can be repeated with new red or white varieties. Once some dexterity is acquired blends from different producers can be included, what really matters is our personal, non-transferable palate.

Tasting

This may be the most important chapter in the *Handbook* as it tries to give some sensible and understandable answers to down-to-Earth questions meant for those seeking them in its pages. Other chapters attempt to introduce the reader to what could be called wine culture, which encompasses the environment of this seductive beverage irradiating a magnetism that induces wine-lovers into an ongoing quest for some more knowledge.

If we have chosen the term "tasting" instead of "sampling" (rigorously speaking a contextual synonym) it is because the latter has a more technical, professional sense. It denotes a more global process than mere tasting and might be closer to the average wine lover. We shall see, however, that tasting—or sampling— a wine is not more than drinking it with all our attention committed to this action.

In a book of his, the already quoted expert Hugh Johnson expresses that: "Too much god quality wine, even great, is wasted. It flows on tongues, through throats unsynchronized with it, non-receptive to what it can offer them. People worried or immersed in a conversation who have just taken a strong alcoholic beverage that numbed their sense of taste, or have gobbled some salad with vinegar that overwhelmed it; who are having a cold or who simply ignore

Aroma.

the very difference between an ordinary wine and a great one. There is nothing a winemaker can do to eliminate the need for a sensitive or interested drinker".

To summarize, tasting consists of transforming an ordinary gesture into a reflexive action. Let's resort to metaphor: reading a novel is not the same as reading an essay. As we try tasting a wine we attempt to extract the most of its secrets, which it won't let go with one plain sip. It is an inquiry about what experts call organoleptic characteristics, in plain English: "for dummies", i.e. an operation based upon the strictly sensory: colour, aroma, flavour, the sort of chemical and physical stimuli that finally get processed by our brain.

In the premises of wine companies the tasting room is the true embodiment of austerity. We will need no more than a table and set of comfortable chairs, some tasting cups, fresh water, a white background, a room temperature of approximately 18 °C and good lighting. Finally, a sampling form where we will write down our opinion.

Colour.

Taste/flavour.

Art not science

Wine tasting has the characteristics of an art rather than those of a science since it means putting wine to the analysis by our senses, what emerges from this experience shall be eminently subjective, unlikely provable.

According to technical manuals several factors are involved in wine tasting/sampling, namely:

• Agent —rigorously speaking— a stimulus, i.e. a physico-chemical process triggering an excitative response in a target organ, the sensory receptor.

• Sensation, i.e. a subjective phenomenon consisting of a response or reflex elicited by stimulation of senses.

• Perception: the final stage, that is sensory awareness or interpretation of sensation.

This latter stage obviously demands a certain learning to allow for a lucid interpretation, the only way tasting can attain a measure of objectivity.

When we say that a given wine is "good", the definition of this term lies along a meridian of personal appraisal. On the other hand, as we call it "dry" or "astringent" our opinion becomes objective because such concepts can be shared from an impersonal, or less personal pattern.

As we taste a wine we should watch it to define its appearance and colour, smell it for his aromas, taste it for flavours and aftertaste, achieving in the end a global appraisal.

To summarize: tasting a wine means paying it a minimum attention while involving our senses.

Colour

The first step in tasting ceremony is wine colour, its optical or visual appearance. The colour of wine is best sensed with natural lighting since artificial light —particularly fluorescent— may prove deceptive.

Colour fluctuates according to different variables: grape variety; manufacturing process; time of contact between peel and must; handling, i.e. stay in wood (oak vats or casks) or lack thereof; total age (wood + bottle); Sun's ripening action on grapes; and way of storage in the producer's cellar, selling point and our place.

Colour spectrum is considerably broader in red wines than in whites since it acquires different hues with passing time.

In red wine we can find ruby to garnet red, the purple, finally black. Factors determining these characteristics have to do with manufacturing process, type of variety and region of origin. A wine's youth or development is determined by passing of time. The reflections or meniscus of a young wine are violaceous to bluish. As time goes by the meniscus will turn salmon pink, finally to a tile-brick hue.

For white wines the palette is a little less generous; we shall find pale yellow progressing to golden-yellow, then straw or canary-yellow, finally, after long evolution, ocher and copper. Marking youth or evolution we will find greenish, golden and bronze reflections, respectively. Low temperature currently used in good white wine allows us to enjoy fresh, very transparent products that preserve very pleasant fruity, flowery or spicy flavours. Veiled wines, i.e. slightly turbid are hard to find nowadays, quite a frequent flaw some decades ago. Today's filtering processes have overruled this possibility. It should be pointed out, however, that in some special white wines e.g. sherry or manzanilla, we can find golden, often even amber hues.

In some white wines of high transparency tiny bubbles can be seen ascending to the surface in a way that resembles low-pressure sparkling wine. This can be due to a wine flaw—incomplete or wrongly-directed fermentation— or to a proper feature of such wines (presence of small quantities of carbon dioxide). Such wines are called *pétillant* in France and *de aguja* [Sp., lit.: "needle wines"], this subtle bubbling rendering them pleasant to the palate.

White wines start darkening due to oxidation produced by heat or light. Their greenish reflections are indicative of greater acidity, regardless the grape variety.

In rosy wines the hues we can observe are pink, dull-pink and cherry (all of them ruby); turning brownish as they age.

Two important aspects are wine intensity and clarity. The former may vary from intense to weak colour, while clarity (or transparency) indicates a good wine, turbidity pointing to problems during its manufacture.

Aroma

Just as eyesight is the sense to judge a wine's colour and hue, smell presides the stage for aroma, called *bouquet* by the French. Are both terms synonymous? Apparently yes, since many experts employ the words interchangeably; however, as a matter of fact *bouquet* seems to have a somewhat different connotation meaning something like an already gauged aroma. Smell is an essential element from the wine-tasting point of view. Somebody called it "a sentry that guards the palate from many surprises". So much of that in the plants of many traditional producers, foremen use their sense of smell to monitor the evolution of the contents of casks or pools.

The truth is that wine *bouquet* is generally an extremely complex set of olfactory sensations caught by people who have this sense well-developed and trained. It's good to remember that tongue an palate—the organs of taste—cannot distinguish so many tastes as aromas can be perceived by smell.

The famous French *nez* (noses) working in perfume industry are capable of differentiating over a hundred of different aromas. A different gamut or breadth of fragrances can be distinguished by wine experts.

It may be useful to express that a wine's aroma or fragrance advances the palate on a series of very valuable data at the time of final tasting. In other words, wine aroma can tell almost for sure whether the product is good or not. What it cannot do is to quantify the quality it advanced, a feat accomplished by the sense of taste, which is integrated with that of smell.

In his 1825 famous treatise on *Physiology of taste* the eminent gastronome Brillat-Savarin wrote: "I feel inclined to believe the senses of smell and taste to be nothing but a single composite sense, with its laboratory in the mouth and its chimney in the nose".

Wine temperature is a fundamental aspect in *bouquet* appraisal. Cold imprisons fragrances, preventing them from free, full expressing themselves. Only a long training allows the taster to know what lies behind the white or sparkling wine that reaches our mouth at a temperature below 7 ° C. Cold *masks* the best part of volatile substances reaching our nostrils, hence it is relatively easier to decipher the message in the aroma of a red wine coming to us at room temperature. However, this room temperature should range between 16° and 18° C; if higher the wine will appear burning and offensive.

To perceive aroma the goblet—for standardized tasting—must be filled up to its Equator; holding it by its foot/stem a first smelling shall be carried out to determine its characteristics and variety typical traits. Once the wine is profiled the liquid shall be spun with a subtle wrist-twisting action to release volatile elements (secondary and tertiary aromas, and alcohol). Too energetic inhalations are not recommended; instead they should be long and gentle. This first perception will eventually work to classify the classical varieties: *Cabernet*, *Malbec*, *Chardonnay*, *Sauvignon blanc*, etc. If as above expressed the French *nez* can identify a hundred aromas, we can humbly do the same with half a dozen distinct aromas.

Experts distinguish between three types of successive aromas: *primary* or original, typical of young wines; *secondary*, reaching its plenitude thanks to fermentation; and *tertiary*, gradually emerging and developed through years of maturation. Primary flavour resembles the characteristic "press smel", that spreads all over the environment in the season of grape harvest and pressing.

White wine aromas can be classified for easier description as fruity, flowery or herbaceous (e.g. pineapple, peach, pear, mango, banana, lemon, lime and rosy grapefruit; honeysuckle and jasmine; fresh-mowed lawn and rue.)

Aromas of red wine can be fruity, flowery or spicy (e.g. plum, raspberry, strawberry, cherry, currant, cassis and blackberry; rose and violet; pepper, black pepper, sweet peppers, oregano, clove, cinnamon, vanilla and black olive.)

This is a hard chapter where training, concentration and good health of the sense of smell count for advancement in our subject matter.

Red wines may have strawberry-like aroma.

Taste

Taste is the obvious culminating stage in wine tasting since this sense—associated to smell—is the capable of contributing the greatest quantity of stimuli to the cerebral terminals of our nervous system.

Tastebuds on our tongue can distinguish many different tastes, yet physiology has been teaching—for centuries—that there are four primary taste sensations: sour, salty, sweet and bitter, sensed by different groups of buds.

However, while some tastes have enological interests others just don't. A bitter or rather salty taste is pointing to wine defects, not features. It should also be kept in mind that as far as wine is concerned the opposite to "sweet" is "dry", not "bitter". A wine is called dry when it reveals a low content of sugar but in this subtle matter other factors must be taken into account beside sugar titer. Higher acidity will be indeed a correction factor for the sensory impression referred to sugar, when comparing two wines of like sugar content, the one with the highest acidity will taste drier.

Acidity confers nerve and character to white and red wines alike, usually being a key factor in a good proportion of the selection carried out by the consumer. While some people won't tolerate a high acidity, others seek it with priority over other features.

Tasting table in "Azafrán" wine store, Mendoza.

Beyond basic tasting sensations palate is in charge of determining a wine's *body* which is a rather complex concept since it results from the alcoholic content as well as from other elements such as extracts, tannin, glycerin, etc. People usually confuse *body* with *colour* calling a red wine with a garnet-like red a product with good body. However, there are softer-coloured wines with intense, bright hues that have a respectable body.

Another element appraised by taste is a wine's balance, i.e. its harmony between body, acidity, alcoholic content and other chemical features. In generic wines it reports the proper *matching* — or lack thereof—between the different components of the blend.

How should a wine be drunk for proper tasting?

Our tongue tip or lips will tell us whether the temperature is right and whether the wine has a presence or just plain dullness.

Then we take a good sip, keeping it in our mouth for a moment. We inhale some air so the wine can bubble in the middle of our mouth, with a gesture similar to the face we make while sucking through a straw. It's at this moment and during the ensuing gulp when aromas reach our nostrils and we feel like simultaneously drinking and *breathing* the wine. According to their type and quality aromas will remain longer or shorter in the palate-smell complex.

Finally, another important element to the third stage of tasting is the backtaste or aftertaste (the French's *après*) given by the persistence of taste in our mouth. According to this, wines can be *short* or *long*. As we have said this condition is commonly called *après* in France; however, it's also known as *arrière-goût*, French for "posterior taste". What we call backtaste is known in Spain as *acabado* [Sp.: "finishing"]. In all cases we are referring to the memory left on our palate by the wine. It may be full, clean and terse—proper of great wines— or short, small-bodied and unsubstantial.

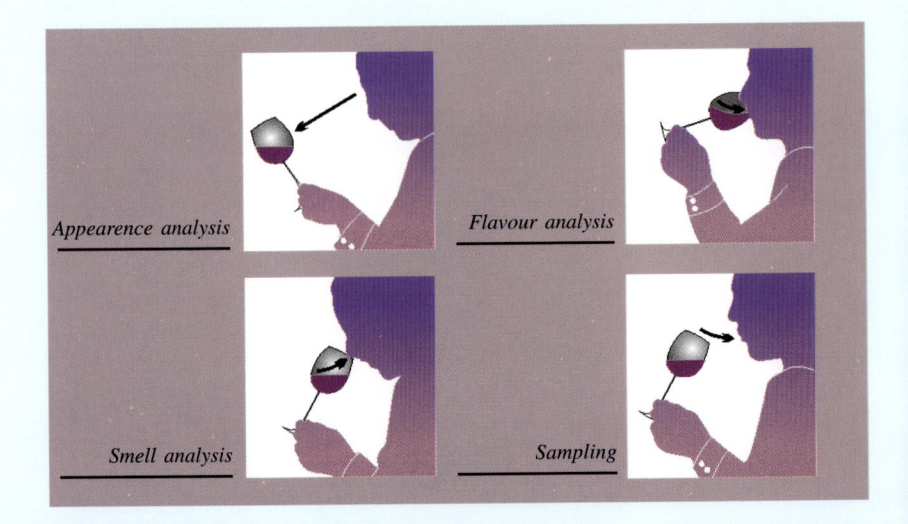

Appearence analysis

Flavour analysis

Smell analysis

Sampling

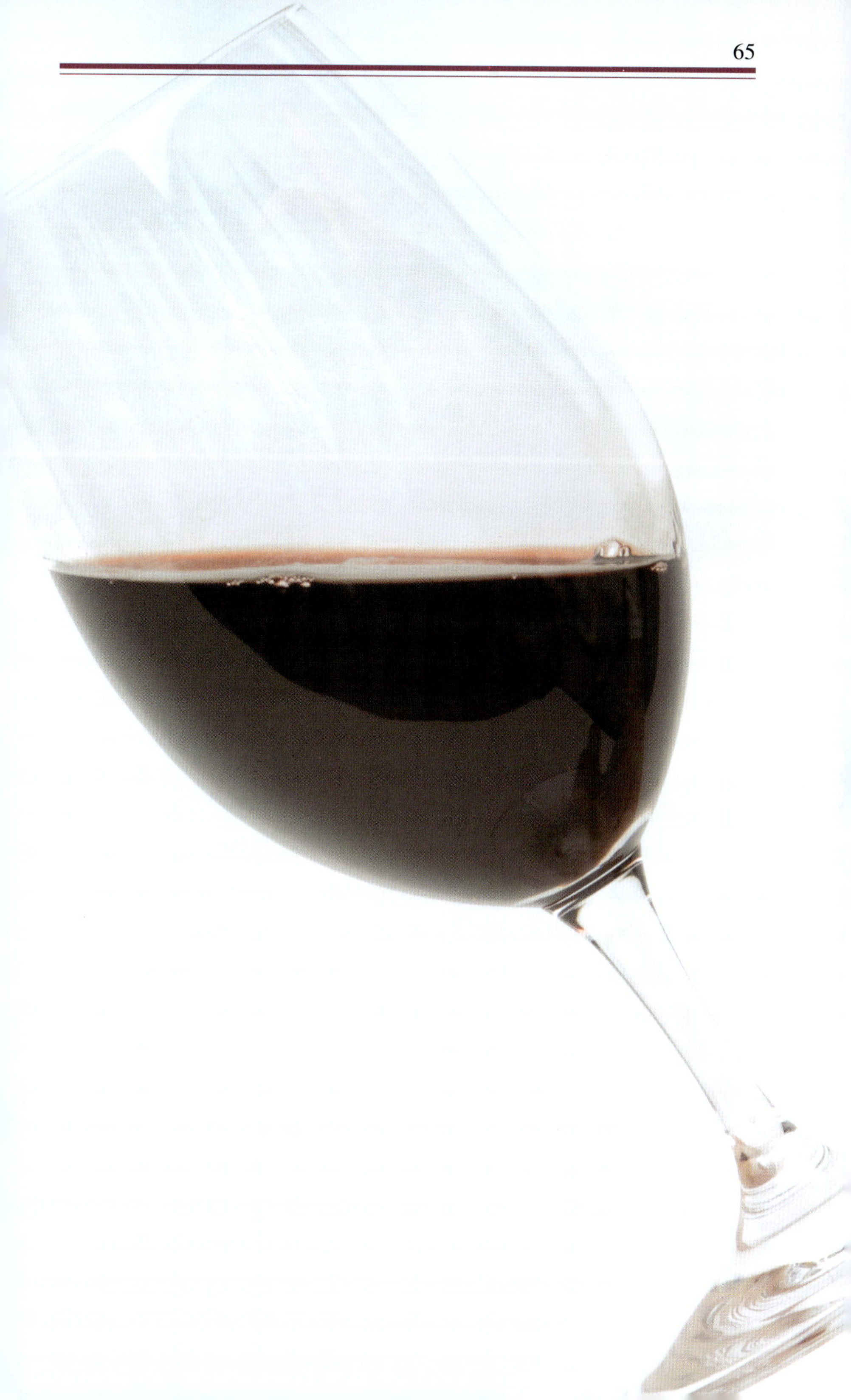

CHAPTER 4

OF PLEASURES AND CEREMONIES

*W*ine requires a translator, an interpreter to "let go" all its virtues, its essence. The right combination is to share it with people with the same passion and mate it with balanced flavours.

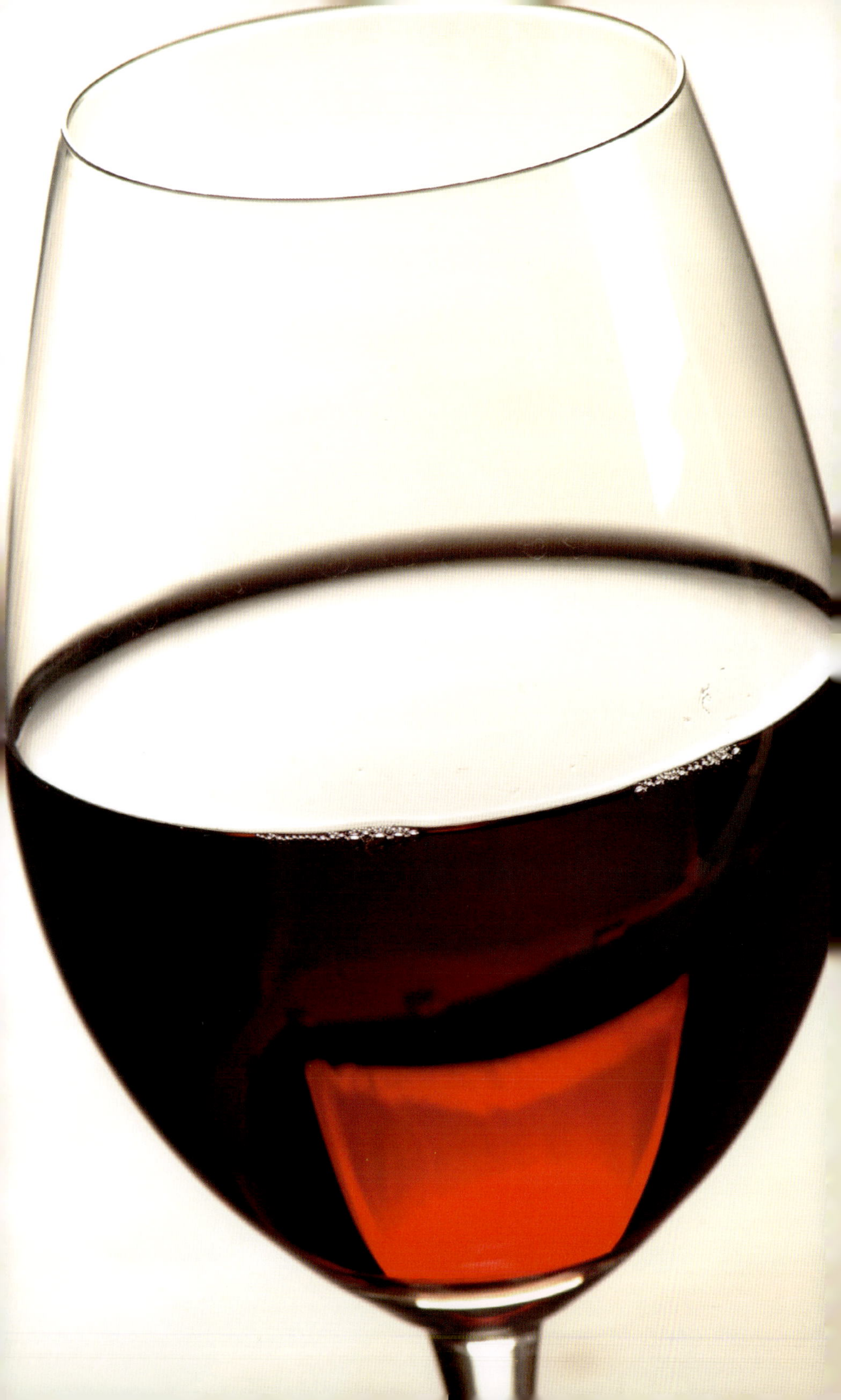

Nobody drinks the same wine twice

Those cautiously approaching knowledge of wine, to whom this *Handbook* is dedicated, should keep in mind a fundamental concept: wine is living matter, hence ever-changing.

What the bottle's glass, a good cork and proper resting places achieve is ensuring the right evolution of a wine, moreover the one designed by its makers; on the other hand they can never freeze in time a taste, an aroma or a colour which will inexorably evolve.

For instance, we have purchased a box with six bottles of red wine. We consume one upon buying and leave the second for six months after, the rest for a longer maturation: one or two years. Those willing to carry out this experiment and have a reasonable tasting memory (a natural talent that can be acquired by training) will agree on the marked difference between the first bottle and the rest. Wine may have perceptibly improved—what is natural—or suffered some deterioration in its quality perhaps because of deficient stowage. What is absolutely impossible is the wine's having remained the same.

Heraclitus of Ephesus, one of the most seductive Pre-Socratic philosophers stated that everything is constantly changing, everything flows. Cold gives way to heat, the day becomes night, big things shrink, small things grow, etc. In support of his theory he produced an attractive aphorism: "No one bathes twice in the same river". Somewhat irreverently paraphrasing Heraclitus we daresay that no one drinks the same wine twice.

Malbec Estrella 1977. Emblematic wine of Bodegas y Cavas de Weinert.

It can surely be argued that this statement is exaggerated, even insolent but through it we tend to show that assertion to hold quite nicely.

We have said that wine is living matter, therefore changeable through time. This condition of wine is one of its most exciting characteristics since it forces us to adopt an almost philosophical stance to it, as well as before life and the spectacle of Nature. No two sunsets are alike to a sensitive spirit even if watched from the same spot on two consecutive days.

To this intrinsic characteristic of wine another peculiarity should be added, the latter inherent to the human being: our perceptual mechanisms are also alive and have the wonderful imperfection of all things human.

The evidence is ready at hand: drink half a bottle of wine at noon, finish it in the evening; then ask yourself if both halves were exactly alike. Almost for sure they weren't. For one, there is the objective reason of the wine's oxygenation after noon; for other because our tastebuds will hardly produce the same response in both occasions.

RJ vineyards, Mendoza.

Happily enough, the computer capable of measuring a wine's virtues or shortcomings has not been invented yet. An immediate, accurate chemical test can be run complete with a thorough answer in written but cybernetics will never be able to tell whether this vintage is better or worse than a previous one.

To a great extent wine participates of those unfathomable mysteries of Nature. In his foreword to *Demian* German poet, essayist and novelist Hermann Hesse (Nobel Prize in Literature, 1946) expressed that "every man is a unique precious essay in Nature". The comparison may sound irreverent but we may say that every bottle of wine is a mystery to unveil, the beginning of a non-transferable personal experience.

Wine and language

All of us interested in the world of wine, who write on it sooner or later face a recurrent problem: how to communicate to others our perception of a series of intrinsic elements of the noble beverage which, as the output of our very senses, prove hard to render objective.

As French wine expert Pierre Bréjoux wrote in the *Revue du Vin de France*: "The first hurdle faced by our samplers consists of finding a wine's qualities and defects, and translating them into a direct, concise language...".

As can be seen this is a universal problem, not personal.

Let's talk about something simple: colour. Can we agree over such terms as crimson, purple, ruby, vermilion, etc.? However, it is not the most conflictive spot since we could find reference in the kind of chromatic palette available for cataloguing colours.

The problem gets more complicated as we move on to smell or taste, description of which is more subjective than for colour.

Another expert—Michael Broadbent—, author of the famous book *Wine Tasting*, tackles this matter, expressing in a paragraph: "What awoke my consciousness [about difficulties] was a series of contradictions by colleagues of mine on a certain occasion. It occurred to me by then that if expert professionals could dissent just like neophytes on a wine's body, lightness, dryness, etc., it could be less a sensory than a semantic matter, or indiscretion in the use of language, or an alarming vagueness".

Based on that crossroads Broadbent advocates "basic" and "fancy" terms, he includes among the former a list of carefully used words, full of sense to samplers or tasters with a modicum of training and experience, e.g. acid, fruity, harsh, nervous, clean, dry, tannic, balanced, etc.

He also lists commonplace terms that should be employed in a limited context, such as muted, fleshy, stout, dense, mature, neutral, dull, rounded, rough, etc.

"Fancy" terms are those permeated by poetry, literature, metaphor and analogy. According to such licenses a wine can remind us of "the grace of silvery willow", "the stately magnificence of purple-leaved beech", "the majesty of oak", etc., if we choose botanical images.

Of course: the closer we get to poetry, the farther away we get from enological precision.

From a semantical point of view it will always be preferable to say that this or that wine has a hint of dried plums or a hogskin aroma, than that it reminds us of southern English countryside or the grace of Delacroix's Tunisian sketches, which takes us back to the starting point. Description of taste leads us into closed languages like those too often employed by certain critics fine arts critics, driving us into perplexity.

If those of us related to wine as simple lovers or eventually *connoîsseurs* we have this language issue, just imagine the one faced by enologists, expert in wine chemistry and manufacture as they try to address consumers. While they can't manage without the technical lexikon and we will never know what "polyphenols" or "malolactic fermentation" really are.

Velázquez, "The Triumph of Bacchus".

Of glasses and temperatures

The act of pouring wine has a ceremonial side, a positively sensible one not to be infringed, for reasons we shall soon understand.

Consider two factors: the "continent" whereby wine is served and the temperature it must have.

There is a non-negligible psychological component to wine-tasting or treating someone to it because it's a detail that renders the act pleasant and worth-remembering. Some people can indeed take high-class wine in plain everyday-service glasses, often tinted. Such glasses are OK for children's drinking water or soft drinks, not designed to house a splendid *Merlot* or a most subtle *Sauvignon blanc*...

Basically a wine will render its whole personality if we take it in a proper glass at the right temperature.

Full sets of carved, quite baroque glassware are still seen in crystal stores with clear glasses only for water, green ones for white wine, ruby or garnet for red wine. They are inadequate since their tint prevents us from seeing the wine's colour, a part of the pleasure of drinking. According to reliable sources, however, such tints have an explanation bordering with fraud: they were created in Europe as some winemakers' initiative because of a persistent turbidity in their wines, conveniently concealed by the artful trick of tinted glass. Such glassware now belongs in museums or cabinets opened only for cleaning purposes.

Goblets made of clay, later metal were used only as ornament but they evolved along with the art of tasting, being Claus Riedel who in 1961 changed the world of wine with his revolutionary concept of the ideal wine-cup. He was the first in History to recognize the effect of wine perception. What differentiates them from other goblets is the crystal's fineness: it determinates visual appreciation, size of body, evaporation area and scent presentation; opening of mouth directs the aroma and essence with the first contact with palate. He designs a goblet for every variety.

It is then preferable to present wine in a fine, smooth uncarved crystal glass, clear, unnotched and undecorated. Hues and reflections of a great wine are thus made visible by tilting the wine-cup. The goblet's body must be separated from its flat base by a thin glass or crystal column enabling us to hold it without heating the wine and allowing an easy rotation (for which purpose the goblet is held by its base). The wine-cup must be filled but slightly above a third of its capacity so that an air chamber is formed on the liquid, where aroma becomes concentrated.

There are different types and the greatest diversity of design. Taller goblets are generally preferred for white wine, jug or tulip-shaped for better appreciation of aroma. Broader goblets are used for red wine, e.g. balloon-shaped for a finer appreciation of pigment nuances.

In a more traditional record we find the sleek silhouette of tall champagne glasses, broader, squat ones like the classic coupe being more commendable than the former as these let scents away. The most elegant sparkling wines cannot be properly tasted in a goblet so open as to prevent our seeing the bubble columns forming.

Glass care

Be careful with the dish-washing machines! Wash your glasses with hot water and cleanse them thoroughly because giant detergent molecules tend to stick to the walls. They shouldn't be dried with kitchen cloths that may leave lint or odours. They are best placed them mouth-down so that water can flow down; a drier can also be used swiftly. Never use detergents to "deep cleanse" a wine-cup, just wine alcohol.

Temperature

The wine temperature issue is a matter of controversy, as personal preferences play a role in it.

I prefer champagne at some 7 °C [45 °F] but many people like it at 10 °C [50 °F], some almost freezing. White wines admit different temperatures according to their type, again, we say that it's neither the expert's orthodoxy not the books that matters, but the drinker's preference.

Wine thermometers are available in the market today and it's OK just to check the temperature of the wine we like. Will our preference be 7° or 9 °C in white or champagne? A little more or a little less? And what about red? There is a broader range here. Some wines are best taken cooled (12-14 °C) such as "blush" and naturally sweetish white. A *Cabernet sauvignon* is not taken at the same temperature as a *Syrah*; the former requires some degrees above the latter to give away the secrets of its palate, usually having a rather complex structure.

It's not recommended to use the refrigerator longer than two days as they may end up damaged, they are best kept in an ice bucket or ice-cold water.

It's said that red wines should be taken *chambré*, erroneously rendered as "at room temperature". The *chambré* dates back to XIX century when temperatures were evidently different from present day. Therefore *chambré* translates best as "cellar temperature" i.e. near 14 - 16 °C. In Argentina, a wine fresh from a restaurant cellar is usually a few degrees below the customer's preference who tells the

Wine preserver. "Azafrán" wine store, Mendoza.

waiter: "Please *chambre* this bottle a little". Of course, there is no such thing in Spanish as a verb *to chambre*. It gives rise, however, to the heresy of dipping a bottle of red wine in a bucket of more-than-warm water. Needless to say, this sudden change of temperature may ruin a wine. A bottle is best uncorked so that it's oxygenated and slowly, not abruptly taken to room temperature.

Hence we say that excessive orthodoxy on the matter fails to match reality; we should do our best about this certainly important matter but never tear our robes if the temperature slips a degree above or below the book. Happily the wine isn't like the human body, where a few hundredths above temperature are enough to give us pain and hardship.

Temperature table for the service of every wine

Variety	Temperature
Red Young red Regular red Great vintage red	Room 12 °C to 15 °C [54-59 °F] 18 °C to 20 °C [64-68 °F] 20 °C [77-86 °F]
White Sweet white Dry white Semi-dry white Spirituous white	Cooled at 6 °C - 15 °C [43-59 °F] 6 °C to 8 °C [43-46 °F] 9 °C to 12 °C [48-54 °F] 10 °C to 13 °C [50-55 °F] 11 °C to 14 °C [52-57 °F]
Rosy	6 °C to 8 °C [43-46 °F]
Sparkling Sparkling sweet Special vintage	Cold 5 °C to 8 °C [41-46 °F] 5 °C to 7 °C [41-45 °F] 6 °C to 8 °C [43-46 °F]

The label, wine's visiting card

Some years ago experts in the Center for Wine Studies depending from INTA's Agropecuary Experimental Station in Mendoza produced a very professional study under the subtitle: *The label as a reference guide to a new viticulture*. It proved almost a prophetic contribution because its advice has been gradually adopted for wine labels since then.

It could be said that some time ago Argentine wine labels were extremely simple, supplying minimum information: the product's brand, the type of wine (reserve, fine, white, red), producer's data (location, registration number, address and little more) only at bottom in a very fine type.

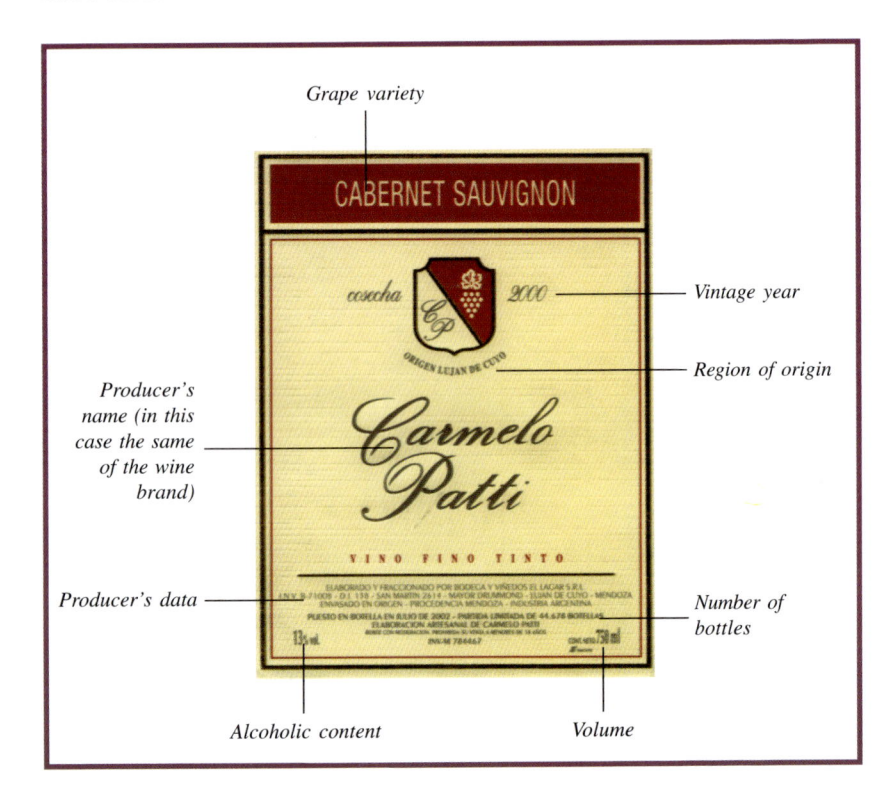

Grape variety

Vintage year

Region of origin

Producer's name (in this case the same of the wine brand)

Producer's data

Number of bottles

Alcoholic content

Volume

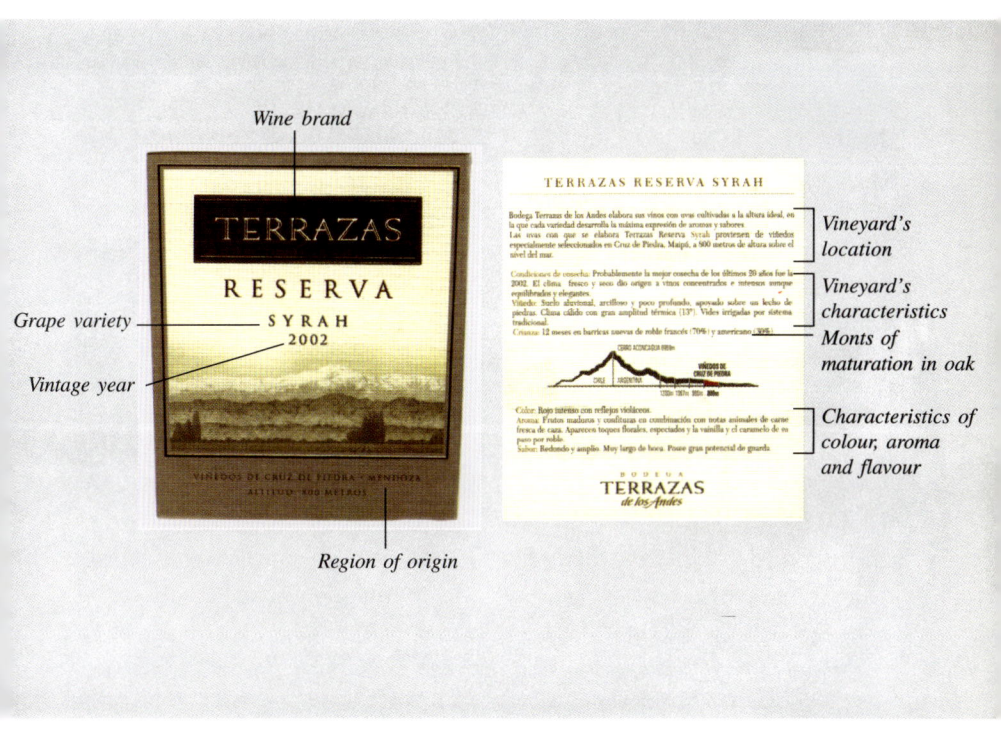

Wine brand
Grape variety
Vintage year
Region of origin

Vineyard's location
Vineyard's characteristics
Monts of maturation in oak
Characteristics of colour, aroma and flavour

This has changed today to the benefit of the consumer who desires and deserves to be informed. Besides offering more information, producers jealously cultivate some aesthetics of their own, generally entrusted to specialized graphic designers, being the label a sort of wine's visiting card it's the first image the consumer gets.

It is then logical for elegance to be sought and achieved, but also that it correspond to the wine's reality. Regrettably it sometimes happen that a good-looking front is nothing but "scenery" meant only to lure the consumer once.

Palate is not so easily seduced as is sight. It could be said that a label, even if dressed by a Christian Dior of *packaging* cannot mask a wine's low quality, just as the most gorgeous binding won't redeem a book's scant literary.

Wines are increasingly adding information to their labels as well as to backlabels on the bottle's opposite face where location of the wine's area of origin can be found in a little map, as well as fundamental data: vintage year, characteristics of the vineyards' soil (in some cases the very name of farms and their addresses).

Perhaps this will be too much information for the impatient reader, to whom what really matters is wine taste, the rest being nothing but literature or some subtle form of advertising. We agree that wine is fundamental but the rest has to do with wine culture that, we insist, is still fundamental to understand that magic of wine referred above.

The label must indicate the region of origin; if possible this will be illustrated in the back label. This way the consumer will start appreciating the differences offered by diverse regions, getting to know Cafayate's sandy soil at 1,500 m [4,920 ft.] above sea level; and Chilecito beneath La Rioja's scorching Sun. Or the remarkably delicate perfume of the *Torrontés* produced in both locations, matchless to that from anywhere else in the country.

Moving on to the South he or she will find Valle del Tullum in San Juan, with undeniable conditions for the production of generous or liquorous wine, the Moscatel-type outstanding for their levels of scent.

Then comes the Upper Mendoza river (mainly Luján de Cuyo and

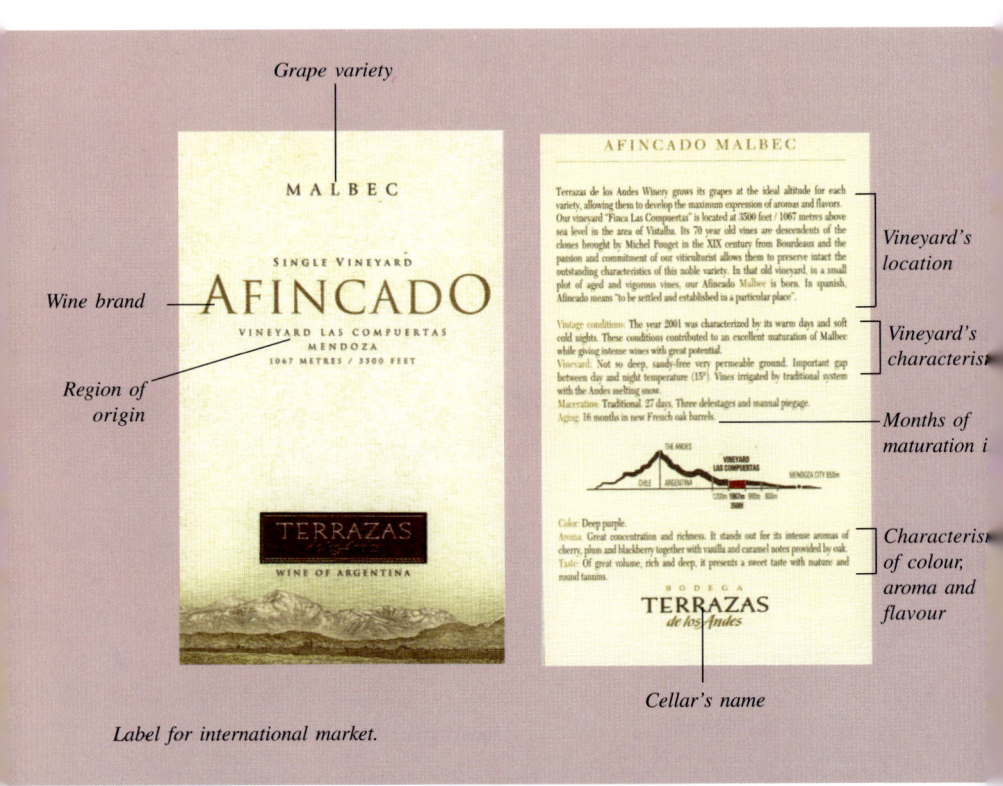

Label for international market.

Wine brand — SAN TELMO

Alcoholic content — 12,80% Alc.Vol.

Vino Fino Tinto
Producción Argentina

Cont.Neto 750 ML — **Content of the bottle**

Cabernet Sauvignon — **Grape variety**
1999

Vintage year

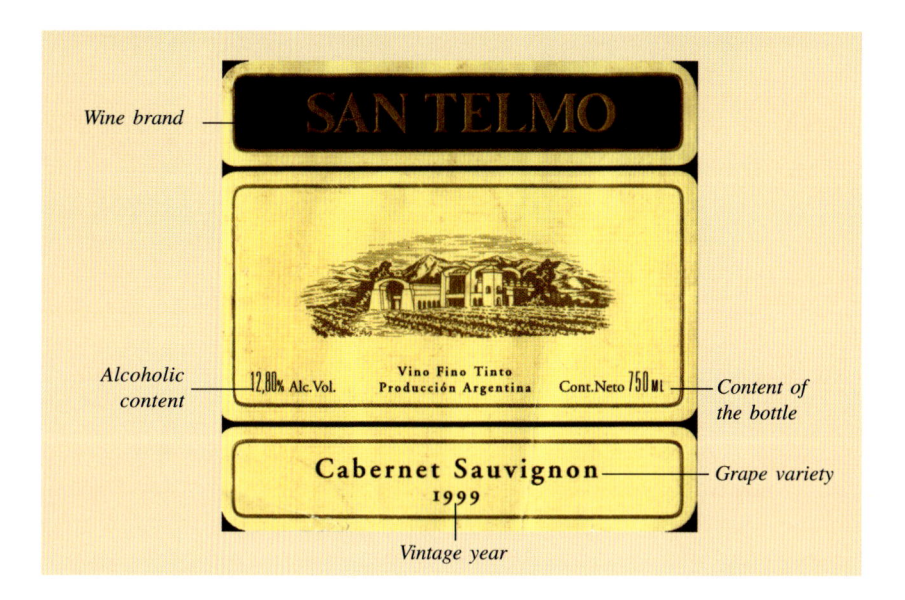

Maipú departments) where the *Malbec* variety found its habitat yielding its best wines worldwide.

The consumer will learn that by ascending more than 1,100 m [3,610 ft.] the Valle de Uco can be found (Tunuyán, Tupungato and San Carlos) where *Sémillon* undergoes a remarkable metamorphose that transforms the worn-out wine of lowlands into the nervous, botanical scented wine of that valley. Also, that red grapes yield abundantly-coloured wine, all this reflecting this land's high-insulation days and cool nights.

Or that areas in Mendoza's East (San Martín, Rivadavia, etc.) and South (San Rafael and General Alvear) are the home of white wines of excellent manufacture with a characteristic regional touch.

Finally the world's southernmost vineyards at 40° S will reveal themselves, with their quality joined to a remarkably typical character, the valley of Río Negro where first-class red and white wines are made.

The back label has been incorporating the vineyards' site of origin, the variety used, vintage year, bottling month and year, alcohol content, serving temperature, organoleptic qualities and whether it was maturated in wooden casks.

Let's keep in mind that the more information the label gives us, the better.

The cork

Cork is produced by an oak species—for this reason known as *cork oak*—very common in Spain and Portugal's warm regions, its impermeable bark manually peeled off in a single cylindrical piece approximately every 9 years.

Real cork (not plastic plugs or cheap imitations destined to ordinary wine) must possess two fundamental qualities: flexibility and impermeability. These enable it to perfectly fit the bottleneck, completely obturating it. Not a single organoleptic quality shall escape before opening.

The long-lived cork endures all years that may come and pass, not suffering either from temperature changes; however, it is not infallible. Three external factors can alter it: an excessively dry environment; the bottle's standing for too long instead of lying horizontally; and attack by certain bacteria.

The way to fight the first two factors is obvious: bottles are kept in a damper environment in a horizontal position. Corks are sterilized to counter the attack of bacteria and insect pests, though this measure is sometimes powerless to prevent development of wine-affecting moulds. Hence the term *bouchonné* (corky).

Quality and size of cork plugs helps the wine-maker to determine a wine's life expectancy. Great, maturated wines can use corks a little over 50 mm long [2 in]; for quality wines they have 45 mm [1 3/4 in]. The smaller the cork, the lower the quality. Curiously enough, specialists measure a cork's length in *lines*.

Corks used by Argentine wine companies.

Cork types

Of course not all corks are alike, and different cork types can be recognized. However, the standard diameter is 24 mm [1 in], compressed to 18,5 mm [3/4 in] before insertion.

Cork types	Characteristics
1. Long corks	Destined to top producers, capable of protecting wine through decades' long aging.
2. Short corks	Employed in shorter-lived wines.
3. Agglomerate	Made of amalgamated pieces of cork, for regular and some sparkling wines.
4. Sparkling wine	They have a long piece of agglomerate plug under which two layers of non-agglomerate cork are glued (the only ones in touch with the liquid). The reason for their mushroom shape is that only the bottom is compressed.

Different cork types.

The origin of cork

Primitive wine amphora weren't sealed with cork plugs. Greeks poured a layer of olive oil on top of the wine which preserved it from oxidation. Modern cork was invented by Dom Perignon, the famous monk at Hartvillers Abbey (in the French region of Champagne) one day in XVIII century, tired of bottles' frequent exploding and losing their bubbling contents.

Today artificial substitutes are available that even look like a good cork, and their usage is rapidly growing at least among export wines and medium and low-priced ones.

Artificial plugs are free of microbiological contamination, which beside the fact of their practically equal cost turns them a very attractive solution.

Bottling process.
Bodega Nanni Hnos., Cafayate, Salta.

ATUNGASTA
CATAMARCA
ARGENTINA
Nº 1232
DE 3000 BOTELLAS
1500 mts.
Añejado en barricas de roble francés
2001
Luigi Bosca
D.O.C
LUJAN DE CUYO
MALBEC
VINO TINTO RED WINE
2004
TRUMPETER
FAMILIA RUTINI WINES
EXTRA BRUT
MÉTODO TRADICIONAL
MENDOZA ARGENTINA
VINO ESPUMOSO NATURAL
PRODUCTO DE ARGENTINA
Alc 12,8% v/v 750 mL
FAMILIA CASSONE
FAMILIA RUTINI WINES
PALO ALTO

Wine accessories

There is an extensive series of elements for the care and enjoying of wine that render such work a true art. In some cases they are indispensable, in others ideal for wine lovers.

Corkscrews

Currently there are corkscrews in every format and price; however not all have the same performance.

A good corkscrew must have a handle, a capsule-cutter, a folding support lever and of course a good helix. The handle must be ergonomic, without cutting edges, soft to touch and allow for a good grip.

The most popular corkscrew type in Argentina is called *rabbit*, which allows effortless uncorking of almost any type of bottle. Thanks to its strong helix treated with a high-penetration sliding-dip and its power lever the plug is easily extracted with no need of hand turn at this stage. The lever has a dented wheel to prevent the bottle's moving while uncorking. Manufactured in excellent materials such as carbon fiber, aluminum and steel to achieve a long life.

A novelty in this market is the walled corkscrew, permanently affixed to a place where the consumer uses to drink wine with friends. It brings a sort of lever to uncork the bottle.

If you have a limited budget choose the conventional dual-drive very solid model. The winged model is not recommended as it usually breaks the cork sending small chunks of bark into the wine.

Choice should be guided by best convenience, i.e. the consumer's dexterity, number of bottles opened or simply a particularly attractive design.

Capsule-cutter

A very recent accessory, it speeds up and tidies up the action. Capsules should be cut 1 cm [3/8 in] below the bottle's mouth to ensure a minimum contact with the remaining capsule at the time of service.

Thermometer

Useful to control right temperature of the wine in the goblet, the thermometer usually comes in a wooden box with indication of serving temperature. Its way of use is quite simple: just place the thermometer inside the cup and read the temperature. For red wines 18 °C [64 °F] is ideal, 12 °C [54 °F] for whites (allowing for some small variation according to personal preferences).

Those most sophisticated prefer an electronic thermometer, which consists of a sort of probe that accurately measures and indicates the temperature inside a freshly-opened bottle. It is introduced in the bottleneck or inside the glass, indicating whether the wine is too hot, too cold or at an ideal temperature.

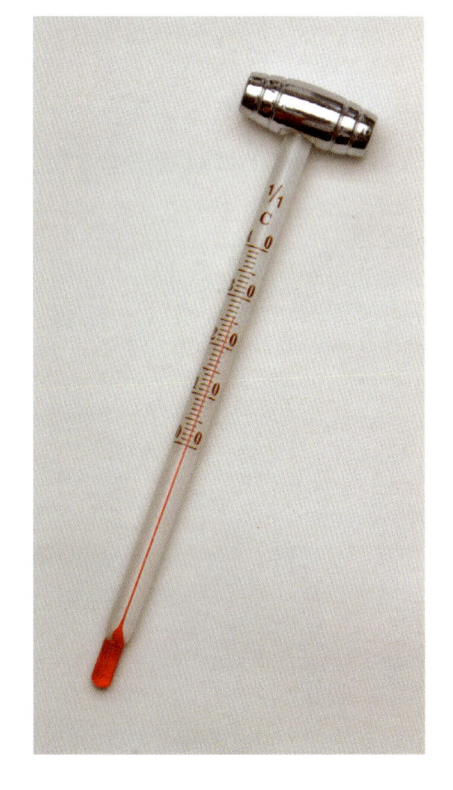

Drop-ring

Not a single drop will stain your tablecloth if you out this ring around the bottleneck. It comes in different presentations: metal, wood, etc.

Drop-Stop

A simple yet effective device, it consists of a simple strip of very thin-aluminum coiled into a tube inside the bottleneck to avoid dripping outside.

Vacuum wine saver

Different types of plugs to preserve wine are available in the marketplace. Some also have an anti-dripping beak. As the bottom is placed on the bottle mouth, its firm and tight grip should be ensured so that air can't get inside and the wine is preserved in a better condition.

Vacuum pumps also belong into this category, they play a fundamental role in storage of a bottle's leftovers. By extracting oxidating air, a small pump allows preservation of the product in a good condition for many days.

Decanter

This glass container is ideal for red wines since some are not filtered while aged wines sometimes accumulate precipitates of tannins and pigments as time goes by. To eliminate these put the bottle in a vertical position a while before uncorking it so that sediment falls to the bottom; after uncorking, pour wine carefully and steadily into the decanter to oxygenate the good reds. Once decanted, vigorously shake the decanter so that the wine's can complete its oxygenation.

Climatized cellars

If not enough space for a cellar is available and there isn't a great number of bottles, climatized cellars are the ideal solution to keep wine in the right environmental conditions. All cellars have specifically designed system for temperature regulation. They are expensive but their design is fit to keep bottles within sight.
Sensitivity and accuracy of thermostats allow for the compressor's or the resistor's working at the right timing as quick as possible to keep an outer temperature comprised between 0 °C and 30 °C with a maximum fluctuation of aproximately 1 °C inside the cellar.

Matching between wine and food

Those of us who approach the wine for pleasure or seeking a healthy training know that this matter is open to debate which can lead us into labyrinthic paths, driven by information, interest, imagination, and above all, controversy.

This because the wine is a matter of personal opinion as are music, arts, philosophy, colour, landscape, mood and all other topics or concepts not amenable to quantitative measurement for want of some universally accepted standard.

While perusing our collection of books on wine, gathered through years and travels, it's quite curious to appreciate the quantity of controversial concepts or terms yielded by enological literature. For instance: what wines are taken with what foods; whether red wines should be uncorked some minutes or hours previous to consuming (even whether this very concept should be considered at all); at what age red wine attains the ideal degree of maturity; how they should be cooled or warmed to ideal temperature; which should be their order of precedence in a meal; and what should be left to drink "in their sameness" using an expression coined by Ortega y Gasset, the great Spanish philosopher.

However, as wine tasting goes through our senses and moods it's hard —better, impossible— for this information to be equally processed by very different sensitivities. Nothing is exact, certain, incontrovertible in matters of sensitivity. Who is Ravel's best interpreter, Pierre Monteux, Ansermet, Cluytens, Dutoit, Lorin Maazel?...One emphasizes his vertigo; another stresses sensuality, ornament and detail, or rhythm. All versions are faithful to the score but the results are quite diverse. It's this diversity in artistic sensitivity that produces different yet equally admirable versions. Wine is a score: we, drinkers, are the interpreters and there will be as many opinions as are consumers.

The only principle that should be respected in "matching between food and beverages" is that wine shouldn't "kill" the food, nor the converse. It should also be kept in mind that some foods and ways of preparation are incompatible with wine as they spoil our palate. Such is the case of artichokes, fennel and asparagus due to a substance called cynarine which causes wine to taste metallic and bitter. When taken rare, eggs block our tastebuds thus preventing tasting. There are no incontrovertible truths regarding beverages and foods. Our palate will tell whether they get along and the choice is correct. If not, there is always time to change.

The best choice of wine for every meal can indeed be suggested. Called *agreement* by some and *matching* by others, it's the way to harmonize tastes, a synergy or aroma and colour. A subjective art, it is constantly open to nuances.

Wine	Type of wine	Characteristics
Red wine	Young	Ideal for: roast lamb, chicken or red meat; meat stew, roast veal; cheese of short to medium handling
	Mature	Ideal for: roasted or grilled red meat, high game (deer, wild boar); wild fowl, feathered game, pasta and complex sauces
White wine	Ligh	Ideal for: cooking seafood, lightly-spiced cold meat and soft fish
	With body	Ideal for: grilled seafood, mollusks and strong-tasted fish
	Maturated in wood	Ideal for: very elaborated fish and seafood, roasted red meat and fowl, marinated and smoked specialties
Sweet wine	*Moscato* and late harvest	Ideal for: desserts, *pâtisserie*, fruit, *foie gras* and blue cheese
	Sherry	Ideal for: fried fish, cooked prawn and shrimp, natural ham and sirloin
Champagnes and sparkling	Extra brut, brut, extra sec, sec	Ideal for: starters, seafood, salmon, caviar and oysters
	Demi sec and sweet	Desserts only

In spite of the above suggestions, if we like e.g. butter pasta with white wine or a rice and seafood stew with a good light-bodied red, then let's go ahead! No Purgatory is awaiting us for such sins.

How to set up your own cellar

Those of us who revere wine as one of the most remarkable beverages created by human spirit use to dream of having a cellar at home—more or less roomy, conveniently ventilated—to build up our own wine collection there. A quiet, austere place where we would allow only friends who share our sort of enological "religion".

Regrettably enough, these times is almost impossible to have a house with a cellar. Only stately houses in the suburbs or some exclusive country clubs can boast of a place like the one we are describing.

We should keep in mind that for a wine to transform, enhancing the complexity of its aromas and flavours, stabilizing its colour, rounding its tannins and harmonizing its structure it's indispensable to respect its maturing and aging. This way its elaboration qualities will be improved.

The place destined for storage of wine may not have all the qualities of a proper cellar but a space in the house can nevertheless be conditioned for it to be kept safely.

The most important for wine storage is previous verification if it has the essential characteristics for aging, it should be tasted, hence several bottles should be available, as well as sufficient information (handling in casks, vintage year, sensory aspects: aromas, texture and taste).

Five conditions for better keeping

The place: It shouldn't have wide variations in temperature, ideally constant at 16 °C [60 °F] to 18 °C [64 °F]. Currently, bottles may be placed inside special refrigerators regulated and tempered as needed.

Position: Bottles should lie horizontally, even sparkling wines as the cork is the principal barrier between wine and oxygen so it must be well-moistened to avoid its drying and prevent oxygen from permeating inside.

Environment: Wine must be guarded from strong noise, aggressive or intense odours, cigar smoke as well as keep enough moisture for the cork's well-functioning.

Light: Bottles destined for aging are generally dark-coloured —brown, amber or green— so the place should have a dim light, not focused on the bottles.

Notebook: We should keep a record of the product's qualities which must include data on vintage, producer, variety, alcoholic content, handling and specific tasting information. As a suggestion, when you have many bottles of a same vintage we should try one every year to prevent it from fading away or to spot the optimum time.

Other important data for wine keeping is knowing which wines are fit for aging. These have body and structure, a good alcohol content, abundant tannins, and good acidity; wood handling also helps.

We should be more careful with white wines since they are less fit for prolonged aging due to their short contact with peel and seed. Nowadays fermentation in casks favours their positive in-bottle evolution, adding a favourable quality for aging.

Chardonnay and *Sémillon* are among the most recommended varieties due to their qualities.

Chapter 5

Champagne, the prince of wines

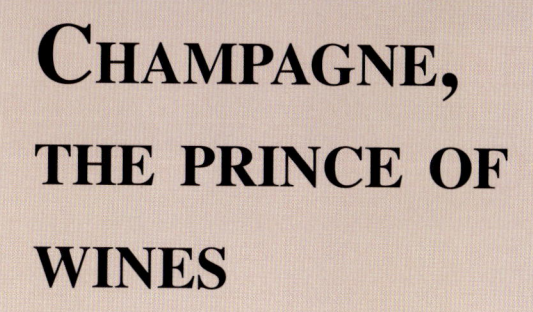

*F*rom its creation by monk Dom Perignon to present day champagne, the starry wine, has been giving us sparks of light in our cup and adorning every important moment in our lives.

ROSELL
BOHER

Brut

Méthode
Champenoise

An exquisite and singular beverage

Although calling champagne "the prince of wines" is a trodden commonplace this doesn't render this expression a trifle less correct. This becomes evident as we take into account the rivers of ink that have flown since Dom Perignon, the illuminated Benedictine monk, practically by chance discovered the *méthode champenoise* of a second in-bottle fermentation exclaiming upon trying his product "I'm drinking stars!" —a beautiful, poetic metaphor to describe its characteristic tongue-tingling bubbles.

Until relatively recently this exquisite sparkling wine has been associated to the ideas of happiness, plenitude, joy, euphoria or celebration. Champagne has always been in charge of toasts and best wishes in weddings, births and New Year festivities. Some time (not more than a decade) ago, however, the lovers of this singular wine realized that its subtle and ecumenical nature was well worth taking advantage in a more everyday fashion, without having to wait for special occasions and the clank of glass.

Today champagne has been given its place among starters since its softness and the joy in its bubbles prepare our palate better than other drinks or cocktails with a force, and alcohol content fit to anesthetize rather than stimulate our tastebuds.

Traditional champagne

Before entering into this matter some clarification is indispensable: champagne is a sparkling wine produced only in the namesake region in northern France. Reims is the capital city to this most noble wine, and Epernay the second city. Sparkling wine produced elsewhere in the world are somehow "usurping" this denomination, even if devoid of fraudulent intention.

The traditional produce of Champagne (France) basic form is elaborated with three variants of the *Pinot*: variety *Noir* (Burgundy's principal), *Meunière* and *Chardonnay*. The former two are red vinified "into white" i.e. removing peel soon enough to avoid pigmentation of must. As we already know *Chardonnay* is white; when the champagne is made only of this latter grape the French call it *blanc de blancs*.

Method for exclusive champagne

All great French brands as well as many in our country employ the *champenoise* method, which we shall briefly describe below.

Starting with a basic wine with the blend or *coupage* chosen by the manufacturer, such elements as sugar and selected yeasts are then added; it's bottled and covered. There starts the secondary fermentation which lasts for several months raising wine pressure to six atmospheres which results in several bottles' exploding. At this stage the wine starts to clarify. It is then moved on to benches—hardwood racks— with a slope that keeps bottlenecks downward. Bottles are then rotated by spinning them from their base as slowly as a radio dial, one eighth of a turn a day. This operation called *remuage* in French, may last between six weeks and four months.

With the finishing of the secondary fermentation the *dégorgement* (i.e. disgorging) of the bottle is carried out. Today this operation is done by freezing the bottle neck where sediment accumulates. This sort of "ice cork" is extracted, carrying away silt, yeast and some of the product. This loss is compensated by adding more of the same basic wine along with bottling dosage composed by aged champagne, crystal sugar, even cognac. The type of champagne obtained depends upon the quantity of bottling dosage added: nature, extra brut, brut, dry, demi-sec or sweet. The driest ones have a lesser proportion of sugar than the sweet. It should be pointed out that drier champagnes (nature through brut) are used to accompany food. The rest are in charge of "watering" desserts, or toasting the end of a meal since a palate spoiled by diverse types of food is not in a proper condition to appreciate a drier champagne.

After disgorging and the addition of bottling dosage comes definitive corking, which calls for high quality corks (some have three layers of different cork so well stuck together that the untrained eye will fail to distinguish the joints). The wire or muzzle works by holding the cork (under considerable pressure) avoiding spontaneous uncorking. Cork wall in contact with the bottle neck is often embedded in paraffin for an easier, non-traumatic uncorking. Years ago the disgorging operation was quite "wilder" than today since the bottle neck was severed by the well-aimed hit of a sharp cutlass inflicted by an expert "executioner". Needless to say, the liquid had to be transferred into a new bottle and the loss of product was considerably greater than with the benefit of present-day technology.

Argentine sparkling wine

The variety most often used for good local champagne is *Chardonnay* blended with *Ugni blanc*, *Chenin* and in some cases *Riesling*.

Argentina has been making champagne for a long time. Back in the *Belle Époque* the well-to-do only drank French *champagne*, particularly three well-known prestigious brands: Pommery, Moët & Chandon and Veuve-Clicquot.

Another manufacturing method is known as *charmat*, differentiated from the *champenoise* as the secondary fermentation after addition of bottling dosage is not carried out inside the bottle but in a big vat. It is then cooled, filtered and pressure-transferred into a second vat where the bottling dosage is added prior to bottling.

According to the quantity of sugar incorporated they are classified into:

Brut nature: no sugar added

Extra brut: up to 6 g/ liter [*0.8 oz/gal*]

Brut: up to 15 g/ liter [*2.0 oz/gal*]

Extra-dry: 12 to 20 g/ liter [*1.6 - 2.7 oz/gal*]

Dry: 17 to 35 g/ liter [*2.3 - 4.7 oz/gal*]

Demi-sec: 33 to 55 g/ liter [*4.4 - 7.3 oz/gal*]

Sweet: over 50 g/ liter [*6.7 oz/gal*]

This sparkling wine changes its name according to the region or denomination of origin, being entitled to the name "champagne" only those produced in the Champagne region in France.

They are called *cava* in Spain, *spumante* in Italy, *Sekt* in Germany, and *vino espumoso* [sparkling wine] in Argentina. The English term has also been adopted as the correct generic denomination.

How to taste sparkling wine?

Several factors come into play when tasting a sparkling wine: goblet and bubbles, colour, aroma, touch and balance.

It is very important to pour up to mid-height of a flute or tasting goblet to observe bubble size and arrangement after settling; they must be tiny, even-sized and form a crown in the upper edge as they ascend. If big and uneven the product is flawed.

The hue should be pale yellow to intense gold, always clear and bright. Bakery aromas from yeast can be appreciated, as well as flowery or fruity scents. Taste is confined to that of a wine but touch has a distinctive trait from bubbling intensity. All the above aspects should evoke a sense of pleasure and balance.

Sparkling wines can be drunk with a starter or accompany a dessert. They are ideal for anticipating a meal, for an appetizer, with seafood or roasted white-fleshed fish as well as different kinds of dessert.

Chapter 6

Wine world: price and quality

The quest for enological quality led to the coining of denominations of origin for better competitiveness in the globalized world. We shall analyze myths and stories about wine where a high price does not always guarantee a consistent height in the quality of its features.

Bodega Cruz de Piedra vineyard.

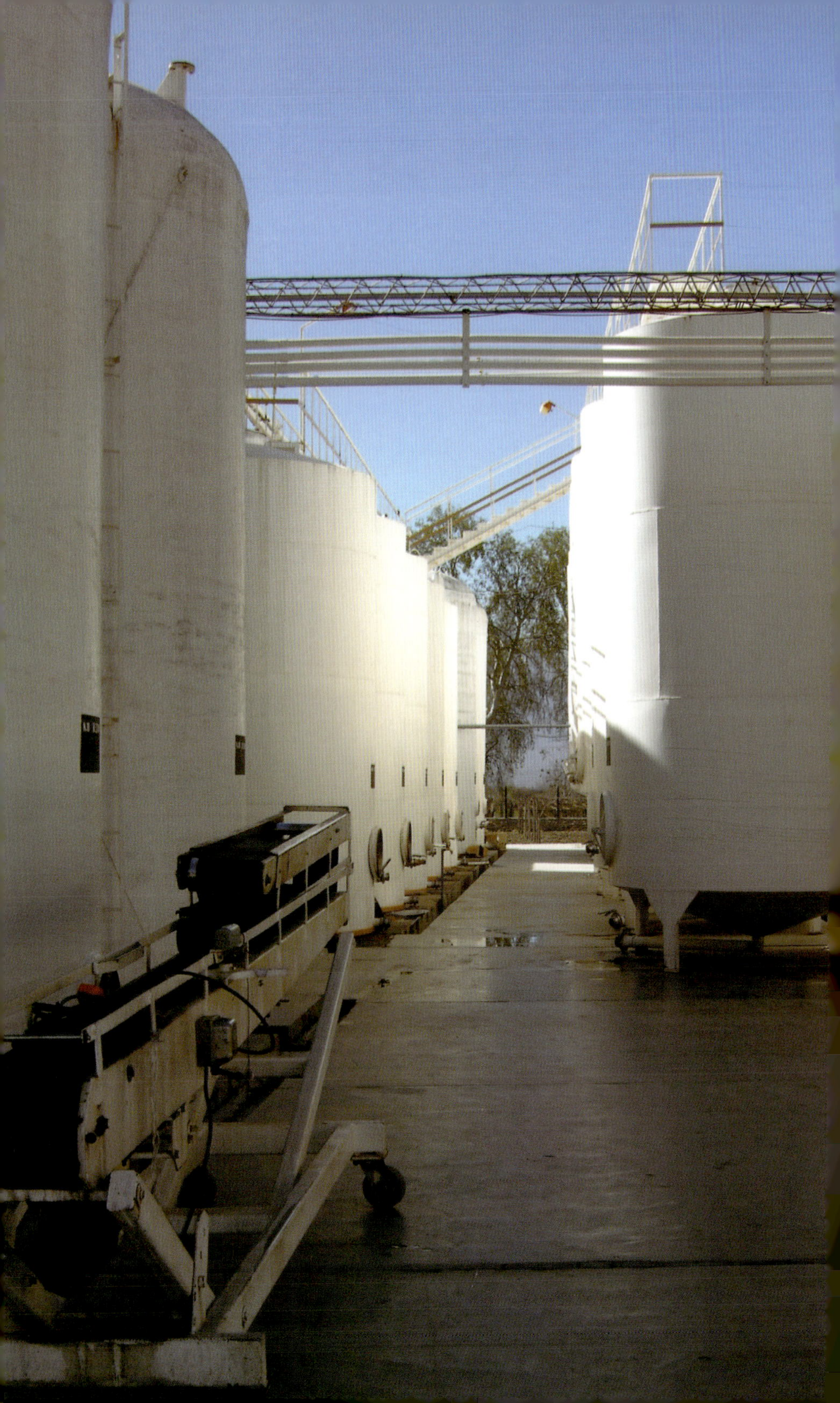

Denomination of origin

In as well as in European countries like France, Italy and Spain, Controlled Denomination of Origin (D.O.C.) for high quality of wine has acquired prestige by the different systems established to regulate certification of the place of origin of varieties employed in wine production.

The foreign consumer is interested in the wine's having passed through the stringent sieve of the D.O.C. certification, a guarantee of seriousness.

Argentina's first D.O.C.s correspond to the areas of Luján de Cuyo, Maipú and San Rafael in Mendoza province, and Valle de Famatina in La Rioja province.

Those wine cellars that have pushed the renowned San Rafael D.O.C. include Bianchi, Suter and Goyenechea, among other important players. They have launched the area's first wines with Controlled Denomination of Origin, with 1992 and 1993 vintages.

Wine labels with denomination of origin (D.O.C.)

In Luján de Cuyo the engineer Alberto Arizu, proprietor of Luigi Bosca and indefatigable seeker of enological excellence, headed the process that led to the establishment of the D.O.C.

As can be seen Argentina seems to be willing to definitively conquer its place in the great world of wine. The D.O.C. issue has not been easy —as nothing is in a proud individualistic country like this— but the steps taken show firmness and determination.

Let's agree that for a wine to achieve D.O.C. quality several factors must concur: natural, technological and human resources. Grapes must be selected respecting their origin, sanity and organoleptic qualities and every piece must express the singular attributes of its soil and climate and being watched by impartial trained experts who establish the parameters of quality and authenticity to enable their certification.

A wine's D.O.C. certification requires certain enological practices such as strict techniques for culture and harvest; not more than 550 plants per hectare [222 acres] and production must be not greater than 100 hundredweight per hectare [4,460 tons/acre]. It also demands control of fermentation, banning of certain machinery; handling must be one year in cask, another in the bottle. Bottling must take place in plants registered in the production area where the Denomination of Origin belongs.

The whole process is subjected to a continuous control of production premises and finished product. The batch's exact location and identification is first analyzed, then samples are subjected to rigorous analysis followed by organoleptic control by tasting. Batches are rated and once manufacture, handling and aging are evaluated, the last analyses are carried out for definitive rating.

A D.O.C. is a quality feature, a true contract for the trust between producer and consumer. Through official recognition it spares the latter the risks of purchase, i.e. immediate identification of qualities sought in origin, authenticity and production methods.

Control of casks in Bodega Ruca Malén.

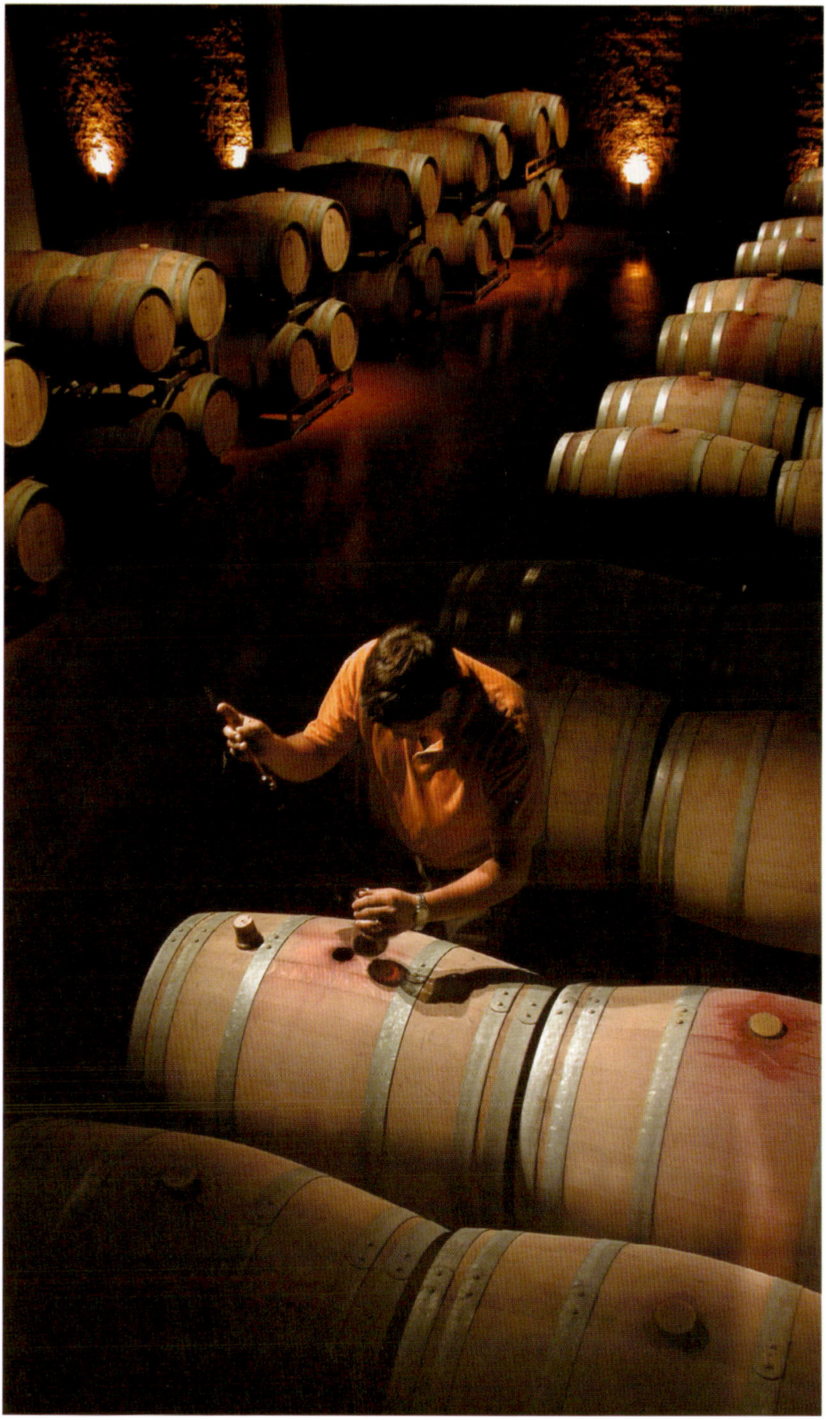

The unavoidable price/quality ratio

Knowing of wines better than the average mortal results in many friends' coming to you in search of your opinion. Their query goes: "Please recommend me a good wine, I'm having some people for dinner". After inquiring about the scheduled menu the following question comes: "How much are you willing to spend per bottle?". This refers to an obvious economical aspect as well as the degree of social commitment to the guests.

It's in this Handbook's aspiration to refer to wine as an object of pleasure rather than a market object; however it's hard, practically impossible, to ignore the price when we talk of quality. When we say that a wine is good or very good, this appreciation entails comparison with its "colleagues" in the same price range, and of course this opinion is embedded in our preferences.

What counts in all cases is the price/quality ratio. Separate consideration of such aspects necessarily leads us into error. In his book *Wine Tasting*, British expert Michael Broadbent points out: "Though not a tasting feature, price is a factor not to be ignored. It's doubtlessly the common denominator of all commercial tasting. Only a snob, a hypocrite or someone awash in opulence will neglect the price factor".

Broadbent later expresses: "For most wine purchasers and consumers, price is the defining criterion since they seek and appreciate the value of what they are paying for as well as quality itself".

Usually, when we purchase wines for our own consumption we choose: everyday wine, wine for occasions of a certain commitment, wine to entertain fine-palated friends etc. These wines we select according to our tastes and preferences, belong into different pricing ranges but in every one of them our experience prevents our neglecting that price/quality concept, in force for every level we choose.

Regarding uncommon wines we can speak of a first layer up to approximately 3,5 u$s encompassing "selection" and "reserve" wines of a certain quality. Obviously this is the range of highest output in times of crisis, with a no-holds-barred fight to establish the top places and leadership. Another range is 3,5 u$s to 5 u$s where we find wines deserving respect, if not all with the same merits. Between 5 u$s and 7 u$s there are wines with a good price/quality ratio along with true intruders in this category. At 7 u$s to 10 u$s the supply is still generous but here we will still find players from quite different categories. Over 10 u$s there is still ample supply, we find wines of excellent quality, many of them prize-winners in international contests.

The role of marketing in product positioning led producers to have a wine at the top range, some respecting the most authentic virtues —production, handling and presentation— while others get chosen by the consumer only from their image, disregarding their price/quality ratio.

In private, producers have told me that in the cost of a bottle of middle-priced wine, the contents —that is, wine— is not one of the most relevant factors. The bottle, a good cork, the package's dressing (label, back-label, capsule) plus the corrugated cardboard of boxes, the thin paper to wrap the bottles (less frequent every day), freight, marketing and advertising today call for ongoing revision of costs. Not to mention that big supermarket networks, wineries and liquor stores channel approximately 50% of sales of edibles and the like. The fight for the consumer is ruthless there too.

I think the above reflections on the price/quality ratio are necessary for the consumer to "quicken the brain and awake", following the advice of XV century Spanish poet Jorge Manrique in his famous *Coplas*.

Again we say that this subject somehow escapes the aim of this *Handbook*; however, it's useful to acknowledge that besides initiating in wine tasting it's good to become a smart buyer.

The leading role of liquor stores

There are several protagonists in wine culture, more present than ever among us. At the top are some producers caring day-to-day to offer us high-quality wines.

Our viticultural map is giving us increasingly interesting wines from diverse regions and varieties. The consumer has become a fundamental figure, much more receptive and open to new proposals in wine, in some way overruling the concept of "classical labels".

To a great extent, this opening achieved by the consumer comes from the place where wine is now sought: wineries and liquor stores. Most such places boast a series of ideal requirements for the consumer to find a good display and distribution without vertigo, as well as the right conditions of temperature, lighting and stowage. Exclusive, selected or sold-out products are chosen by the place's qualified personnel. Several initiatives are impelled by the trade such as directed tasting, beginners' courses or selection of new wines with customers by tasting.

Winery in Buenos Aires.

Above all: the indispensable advice of a *sommelier* or expert. These people will give a lot of themselves to make sure the consumer finds not only the wine sought for but also the recommendations in accordance with its best tasting.

Places where to find all the above requirements for beginners, the savvy and the Sybarites are the new wineries that have succeeded in interpreting and attracting the consumer with the right tools, from product choice to additions for ideal enjoyment: glassware, accessories, delicatessen, specialized literature, tasting sessions directed by specialists, courses, etc. Their basic premise is good disposition, kindness and knowledge of regular customers.

Interview with Daniel Dengis

Daniel Dengis has got an MBA and runs a winery in Belgrano quarter in Buenos Aires. With great experience in the wine world and belonging to a family with viticultural tradition, he refers us that the principal tool for such an enterprise is a combination of several ingredients: good training, a trajectory, general culture and a thorough field study.

What are the causes of this winery boom?
Today wineries and liquor stores are imposing themselves because it's there where the wine receives the best care as well as value added of expert advice, guaranteed quality and the possibility for the consumer to deepen his or her own wine culture.

What are the basis for establishing a winery?
It requires very solid foundations as specific training and a wide spectrum of wine-related culture: music, art, literature, etc. Having "a track record in the world of win" also helps before our suppliers/producers and future consumers who accompany us, providing an efficacious group work. Finally, carrying out a thorough field job by identifying the needs and profile of the target consumer.

Can you outline your working strategy?
Fundamentally, a clear choice of my resources to obtain a competitive edge by working with professionals strongly oriented to the customer's needs, whose goal is a faithful consumer while accompanying the market's evolution with appropriate advice.
Regarding internal working dynamics, I start from a participative design so that everyone can understand and accept different outlooks and knowledge, shaping their ideas and developing a framework of understanding for solving problems.

Which are the basic tools for better competitiveness?
The fundamental tools are information systems and technological communication, public relations policies and organizational

structure, e.g. tasting, product launch, bilingual speeches for tourists, beginners' courses in the world of wine, food choice, advising companies etc.

Daniel, does your name have a track record in the viticultural world?
Yes, our family has always tasted reserve wines on different occasions which eventually got us closer to the wine world; a whole lifetime in enological culture.

What do you like best in your business?
The greatest attractive resides in the dynamism of this wonderful world of wine, it gives you surprises every day. Second, the socializing effect from having a wine cup with people who share your passion: comparing, debating, projecting...

APPENDIX

Frequently asked questions

Myth, uncertainty and doubt intertwine in the world of wine at the time of choosing, opening or tasting wine, you'll find the right word.

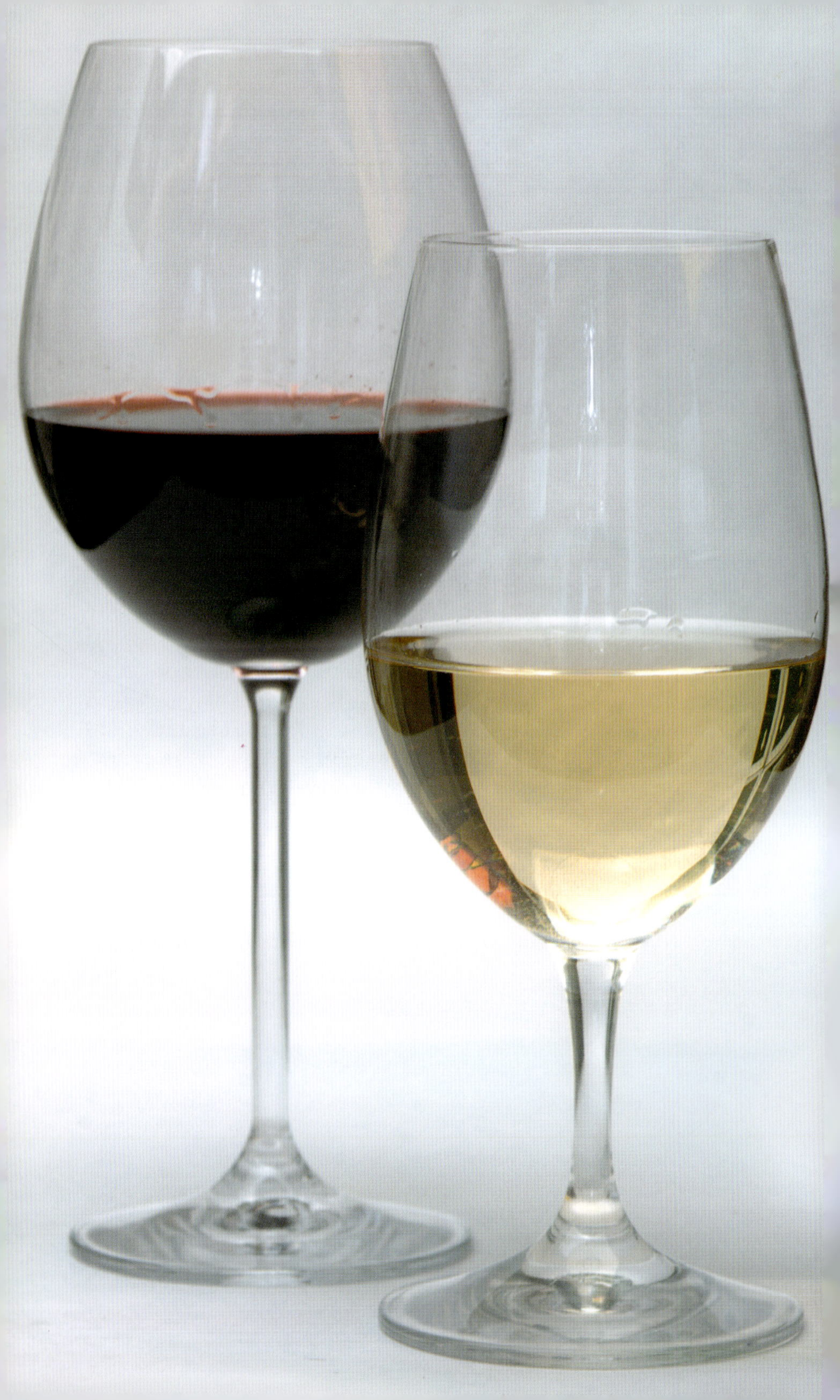

Everything about wines

How should a wine be opened?
The right temperature should be ensured before uncorking.

For aged or many-vintages wine the bottle must stand for a while so that sediment precipitates to the bottom and wine can be served without it.

The steps to open a bottle of wine are the following: remove the top capsule with a capsule-cutter or knife thus avoiding contact of wine with the metal as it flows from the bottle into the goblet. The reason for this is that capsules were formerly made of lead and contact with any metal is not recommended (some experts prefer to extract it completely instead of cutting its top). Wipe the surface of cork and bottle with a cloth, especially if it has been too long in a damp cellar. The cork surface may have a layer of mould but this is nothing serious. It may become a serious issue if wine stains are found in the cork as it may indicate outward leak of wine, with concomitant penetration of oxygen. Drive the corkscrew into the cork's core right to the end, trying to keep it straight. Then carefully extract the cork from the bottle neck.

How does air affect wine?
Wine deteriorates if left exposed to the air, its fruity components oxidating. During the manufacturing process this develops gradually, and for this reason producers take their precautions by minimizing contact of must, fermented wine and aged wine with it, resorting with necessary to inert gas.

How long should the wine "breathe"?
Many wine lovers say that it's necessary to air young wine to speed up the maturing process, allowing molecules responsible for aroma to become more readily sensible by our sense of smell and strong, high-tannin wines to smooth. Decanting of bottles, i.e. pouring their contents into a container, is an effective method for wine airing. The younger the wine, the stronger its need for airing.

Are different goblets required to drink different wines?
Of course, it's not just that two types of wine-cup are needed, i.e. for champagne-type sparkling and another for regular wine. All must be made of plain thin glass, colourless and clear to appreciate the whole spectrum of wine colours. Champagne glasses must be elongated, flute-like to avoid bubble dissipation and enhanced concentration or aromas. Regarding wine goblets, they should have greater capacity for aromatic molecules to concentrate.

How is a dry wine distinguished from a sweet one?
A wine's dryness is due to the absence of sugar. So the contrary is a sweet wine. This is indirectly related to the acidity since sugar masks a wine's acidity so sweet wines seem to have a lower acidity than they really have.

Why is wine an important element in gastronomy?
Because it enhances or improves the natural flavour of food, reduces the use of salt, adds aroma, balances taste and moistens. It is also employed for seasoning.

Wine rapidly evaporates during cooking and the grape's natural flavour is mixed with those of food. As a wine boils down its taste is enhanced, but it will keep its flavour if incorporated towards the end.

How is sparkling wine served?
Sparkling wine or champagnes should be served as appetizers due to their dry character, however they can also accompany starters and main courses, even some desserts.

The bottle should be opened right at the moment when it will be consumed. The right temperature should be verified before, i.e. 6 °C to 10 °C [43-50 °F]. For constant temperature place the bottle in a bucket with water and plenty of ice.

How can wine be uncorked noiselessly?
Hold the bottle at a 45° angle, removing the muzzle (metallic structure covering the cork), then hold the top cork with your thumb so as to stop it if it pops out, holding the sides with your hand. With the other hand spin the bottle. Gradually extract the cork, always holding it firmly;

when it starts popping out pull it inwards to delay its progression. The noise made by the cork should be soft and delicate.

What is oxidated, stingy our mouldy wine?
Oxidation is common in white wine for its excessive contact with air, losing its characteristics and becoming sherry-like in flavour and aroma.

Wine is stingy when attacked by acetic bacteria that transform it into vinegar. Its aroma becomes sour and like acetone (nail-polish remover).

Mouldy taste is not always due to the cork but to compounds (trickloroanisols) contaminating it and all containers in contact with the wine during its elaboration, hence the important of good hygiene in all the plant. Such compounds are non-toxic agents that attack wine's aroma and flavour.

What is the best place to buy wine?
Doubtlessly the winery, where you will find personnel capable of advising you regarding aging time, consumption temperature, good food choice; at the same time you know that the wine was well-tended, i.e. that it didn't suffer sudden temperature changes, rests in a moisture-controlled place, is not exposed to strong lighting or any other factor that can alter it, especially if it is a mature wine to keep in your little cellar.

Salta city cathedral.

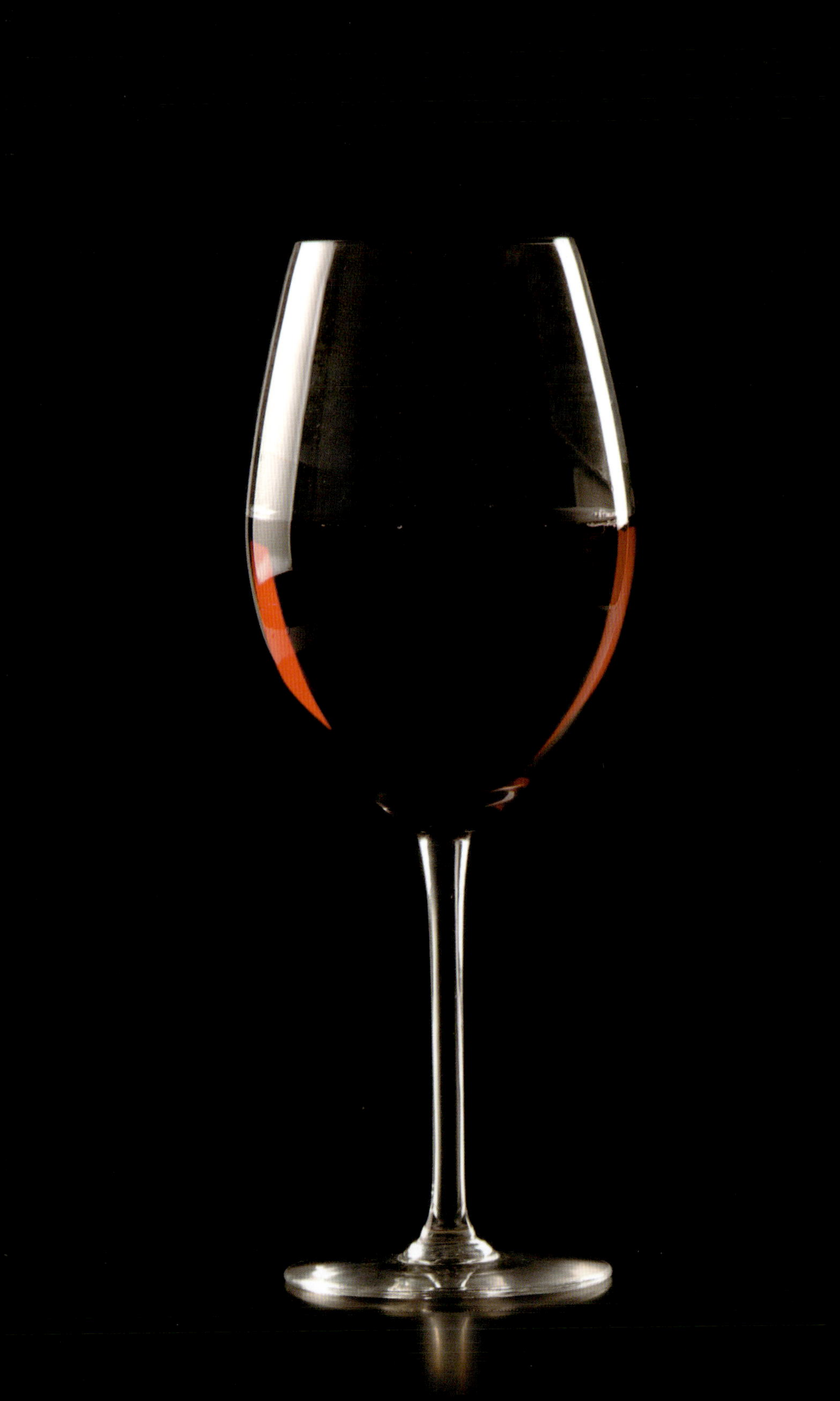

Brief enological dictionary

In a chapter of this *Handbook* we pointed out that wine language frequently recurs to metaphor and analogy to describe aroma and flavour, which are essentially subjective sensations or perceptions. However, nouns and adjectives used in the vinicultural world to define some characteristics or peculiarities of this beverage have quite precise connotations.

We have compiled a brief enological dictionary picking the most extended terms in the abovementioned attempted definition. We include the most usual, from diverse sources of information.

A

Acetic: "stingy", sour, vinegar-like wine.
Acid: the level of acidity becomes excessive and unpleasant. Acidity can be fixed or volatile.
Amontillado: wine characteristic of Jerez (home place of *sherry*), or more properly Montilla, with filbert flavour and considerable body.
Astringent: a feature of certain varieties when young (e.g. *Cabernet sauvignon*). It feels in the gums.

B

Balanced: wine with matching intensity of colour, aroma and flavour.
Bite: quality of a wine rich in body and aroma.
Body: quality of strong wine with a respectable alcoholic content.
Bouquet: French word that designates a set of olfactory sensations offered by a wine aged in bottle.
Breed: high-class, quite representative of its variety and region.
Brief: when the sensation after taste last only a few seconds, i.e. short-lived flavour. Without backtaste.
Bright: it refers to visual qualities. As the cup is spun against a light source, its clarity and transparency become evident.
Brut: sparkling or champagne with very little residual sugar.

C

Caste: high-quality wine, well-handled from its origin.
Classic[al]: a wine whose offspring has endured time.

Coarse: rough, vulgar, low-quality wine.
Cold: wine hard to give away its aromas as if locked into itself.
Complete: balanced, with harmonic visual, aromatic and palatal virtues.
Complex: with many different flavours and aromas.
Corky: tasting like cork (in French *bouchonné*), it's produced when the latter is mouldy.

D

Delicate: fine, pleasant subtle wine, albeit not necessarily distinguished.
Dense: practically synonymous of "rough", devoid of distinctiveness.
Distinguished or elegant: delicate, gentle, drunk with pleasure.
Doughy: mellow; rich in dry extract and glycerin.
Dull: wine without strength, brightness or significant flavour.

E

Easy: gently-drunk wine without sharp edges.

F

Fatty: its high glycerin content confers it unctuosity and gentleness, e.g. the famous Sauternes, a major glory of France.
Flat: without body, flavour or life.
Fleshless: a wine poor in alcohol and dry extract.
Fleshy: consistent, dense, thick wine that communicates the sensation of "chewing" it.
Flint: odour reminding that of flint sparkles observed in some white wines.
Frank: unmistakable wine that gives the palate very precise sensations and well-defined aromas.
Fresh: generally young wines of the year's vintage, easily drunk, not saturating.
Fruity: wines that keep the flavour of fresh grapes or have aromas of other fruits like currant.

G

Gaunt: wine matured or aged past its prime, which has lost the virtues it may have had.
Generous: special wines like Marsala, Port, Mistela, etc., of high alcoholic content.
Gentle: wines rich in glycerin, pleasant to the palate and tingling at the mucoses.
Glyceric: a wine, unctuous to the palate as a consequence of the right content of glycerin.
Green: very young wines of marked acidity, characteristic of Portugal.

H

Hard: wine devoid of gentleness, little pleasant to the palate.
Harsh: astringent, rough, hard to drink.

I

Iodinated: with iodine tincture-like aroma. Found in wines with a long bottle handling.

L

Light: a wine of scanty taste and body, easy to drink.

Liquorous: sweetish, thick wine.
Loaded: thick wine, with intense colour.
Loose: weak, scanty-bodied wine.

M

Mild: sweetish wine, or with a tendency to sweetness. This can be due to added sugar or a natural feature, i.e. by selecting grapes at their highest degree of ripeness.
Mouldy: wine with mould-like flavour and smell, generally the result of handling in a cask deficiently dried after washing.

N

Natural sweet: a wine with a high content of residual sugar resulting from stopping alcoholic fermentation by addition of sulfurous anhydride or some other enological procedure.
Nerve: quality of a wine with enough flavour and body to be stored for a long period while preserving the same degree of quality.
Neutral: undefined wine, devoid of particular characteristics.
Noble: classy wine of high-caste. Also applied to wines of the lower price range but elaborated with dignity.

O

Open: very clear, weakly-coloured wine.
Organic: wine elaborated with a minimum usage of chemicals in culture and manufacturing process.

P

Prickly: slightly sparkling, with remainders of carbon dioxide. Generally pleasant to the palate. Known as *pétillant* in France, the term has been to a certain extent incorporated into English.

Q

Quarrelsome: cheap harsh wine, albeit with character.

R

Raw: wine that has not yet attained its maturity, with remarkable acidity.
Rounded: very well-balanced wine, quite pleasant to the palate. Generally rich in alcohol, glycerin and acidity.

S

Sappy: a wine with marked flavour and aroma. It leaves in the mouth a sensation of splendour, synonymous of optimal maturity.
Sherry-like: flavour of fine wines maturated for too long or with some defect in manufacture or handling. Not equivalent to sour.
Short: wine of scanty taste and fleeting persistence.
Soft: wine devoid of character, acidity, nerve.
Soul: a wine's character or personality.
Sour: wine made of low-quality varieties; harsh, hard, acid.
Sour-cherry: young red wines, perhaps rich in tannin.
Sparkling: wine treated with carbon

dioxide or bottled before the end of its fermentation.
Spirituous: wine rich in alcohol, when drunk generates a sensation of heat in the stomach.
Stingy: "sick" wine, acidulous and turbid, without flavour or strength.
Stout: consistent wine, with a good alcohol content. Synonymous of vigorous and solid.
Strong: spirituous wine, good-bodied, strong-tasted, warm, fiery.
Structure: a series of related essential features of wine, acidity, content of alcohol, tannins, fruit and sugar.
Sulfur: hot-odoured. Low quality wine that has used sulfur as preservative.
Sweet-sour: defective taste of a wine fermented at too high temperature.

T

Tender: of low acidity, light, fresh, pleasant to the senses.

Thin: very light. Not enough winy, insufficient body or character.
Turbid: of poor transparency, opalescent, characteristics almost absent in today's wines.

U

Unbalanced: when its components do not attain harmony of organoleptic characters.

V

Velvety: wine that gently caresses our palate, with little acid, rich in glycerin.

W

Winy: strong, spirituous, sometimes in detriment of fineness or elegance.
Woody: a wine that markedly preserves the flavours and aromas communicated by cask or vat, likely handled in very old wood.

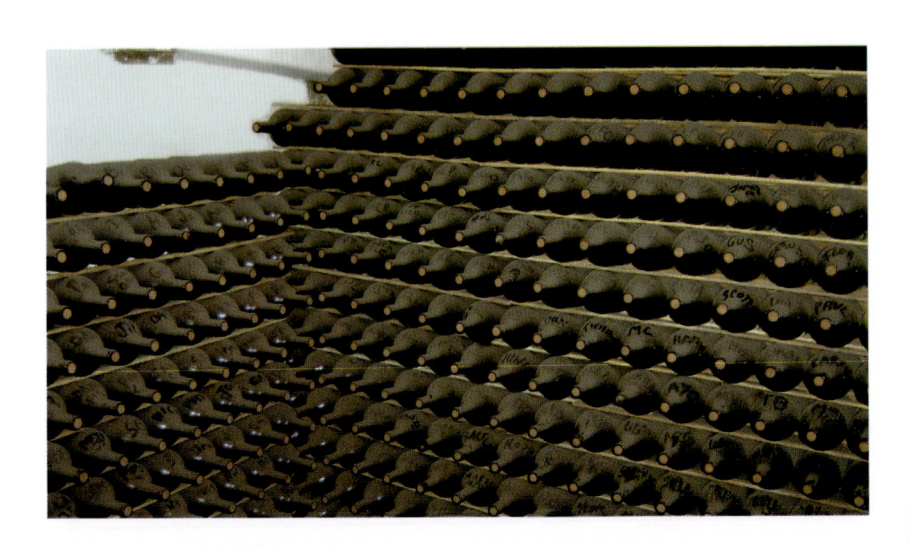

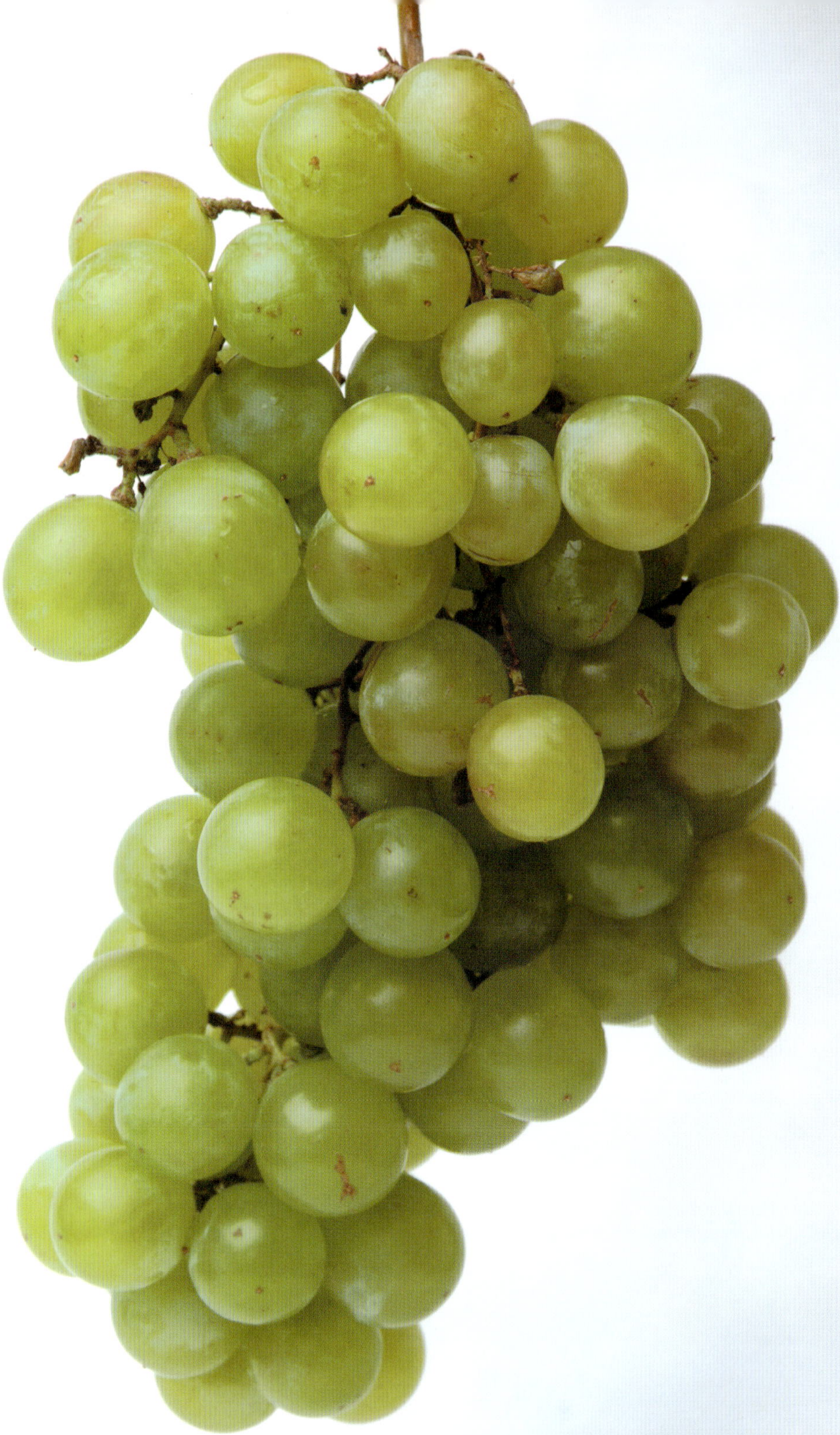

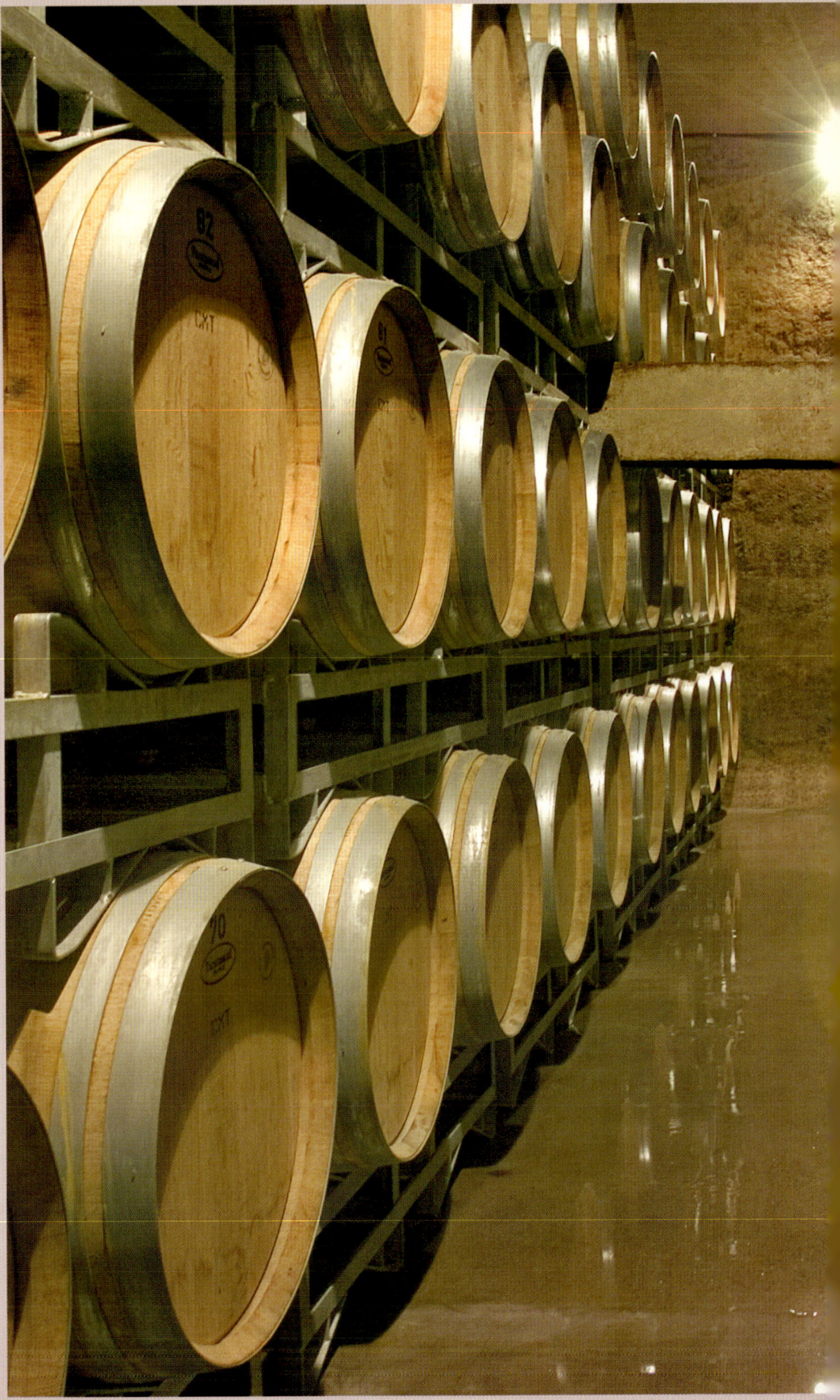
82
CXT
70

Wine companies in Argentina

Touring Argentine vineyards standing beside the imposing Andes range means discovering the expression of the land in every wine.

Casks in RJ wine company.

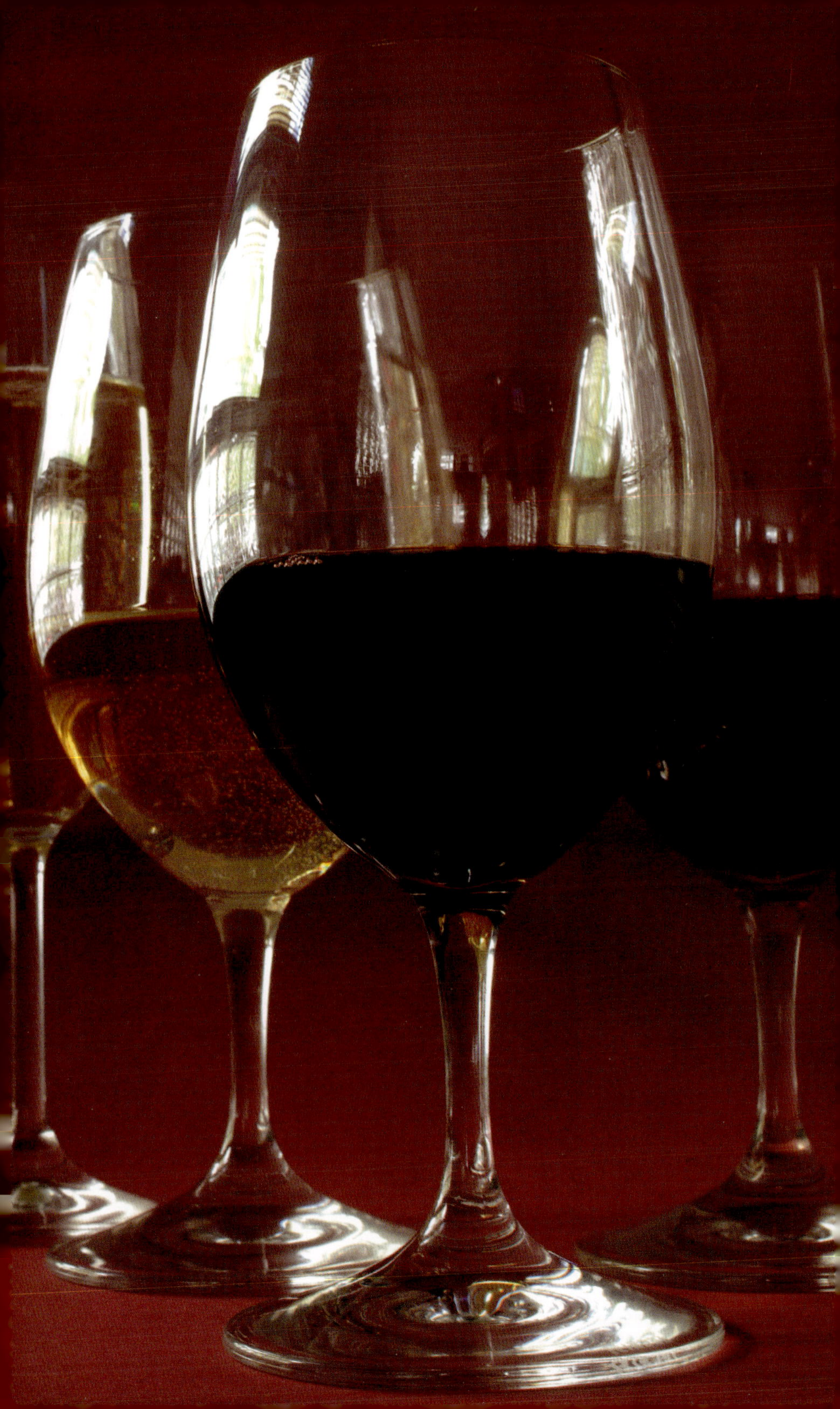

Boutique companies

This term is generally associated with the fashion industry and personal or familiar business, however, today it is a synonym for a sense of quality, craftmanship, customized care.

The development of a *boutique* company calls for a familiar and corporate effort but it needn't have its own vineyards; it's necessary to be able to select the right grapes to produce the desired type of wine.

Such companies were once rated for the volume of wine produced, initially up to 100,000 liters [26,417.2 gal] but as a great number of companies with these characteristics have appeared, today the limit for "boutique" status has increased to 1,000,000 liters [264,172 gal].

Boutique companies are evolving until they become major producers by incorporating more developed technology and production techniques without forgetting their beginnings and success.

Wine selection. Bodega Carmelo Patti. Mendoza.

Bodega y viñedos Nanni. Salta.

MENDOZA

ACHÁVAL-FERRER

A circle of friends in Argentina and Italy joined dreams and efforts in 1998 by undertaking a commitment to respect for quality and terroir. Achával Ferrer is a company located in Mendoza province, only manufacturing high-quality red wine in limited batches. It is a dream rather than a project, the idea of gathering together friends from Argentina, Italy and the rest of the wolrd in a task with the axis of expressing the greatness of the wine of a territory.

Location
Azcuénaga 453 (5507) Luján de Cuyo (Mendoza)

Wines
Finca Altamira, Achaval Ferrer Quimera and Achaval Ferrer

Visits and tasting
With previous notice.

Contact
Phone: (54 261) 498-4874 (54 351) 425-3812
Fax: (54 261) 498-4874
E-mail: ventas@achaval-ferrer.com
Website: www.achaval-ferrer.com

ALTA VISTA

Created in 1997 by Jean Michel Arcaute, one of the most renowned enologists in France twice elected "Winemaker of the Year" (1991 & 1995) by the prestigious journalist Robert Parker. Seeking a *terroir* where to elaborate wines respecting complexity and distinction he chooses to settle in Mendoza. In 1999 the d'Aluan family and their son Patrick enter the project as well as the marketing structure. After Mr Arcaute's tragic demise the Alta Vista company is being led by Patrick d´Aluan. Philosophy with methods usually applied to French *grands crus* are adapted to Argentine terroirs.

Location
Álzaga 3972 (5528) Chacras de Coria - Luján de Cuyo. Mendoza

Wines
Alto, Gran Reserva Terroir Selection, Premium Varietales, Finca Montelindo
Sparkling wines: Atemporal

Contact
Phone: (54 11) 809-3535
E-mail: altavista@altavistawines.com
Website: www.altavistawines.com.ar

BODEGAS Y VIÑEDOS VALENTÍN BIANCHI

Don Valentín Bianchi came to Argentina in the year 1910 from Italy, his original homeland; he founded the famous "champagne company", three generations following his dream. In 1996 the new plant was built on a ravine, accompanying the design with great production and storage capacity.

Location
Route 143 and Calle El Salto (5601). Las Paredes - San Rafael (Mendoza)

Wines
Enzo Bianchi Gran Cru, Famiglia Bianchi, Bianchi Particular, Bianchi 1887, Don Valentín Lacrado, Varietales D.O.C.
Sparkling wines: Bianchi

Visits and tasting
Monday - Saturday 9:00 to 12:30 and 15:00 to 18:30. Free.

Contact
Phone: (54 2627) 435353
E-mail: informes@vbianchi.com
Website: www.vbianchi.com

BODEGA CATENA ZAPATA

Designed according the architectural style of Mayan pyramids, its plant was spatially and technically conceived with the goal of gentle, delicate handling of grapes so as to ensure preservation of natural aromas and flavours in the fruit. This style of admirable grandeur has the intention of symbolically asserting Argentina's position as a wine producer in the world. It is located in a privileged area surrounded by 20 years old vineyards. Starting at its vault, concentrical spaces extend down to the ground. There a circular cell with 4,000 oak wood vats and modern technology support a process destinated to the obtention of great wines.

Location
Calle Cobos s/n (5519) Agrelo - Luján de Cuyo (Mendoza).

Wines
Catena Zapata Estiba Reservada, Angélica Zapata, D.V. Catena, Saint Felicien, Álamos and Uxmal.

Visits and tasting
Wine tasting in tasting-room only by contract.

Contact
Phone: (54 261) 490-0214 / 490-0217
E-mail: catenazapata@interlink.com.ar
Website: www.nicolascatena.com

BODEGAS CHANDON

In 1955 Count Robert Jean de Vogué, President of Moët & Chandon (Epernay, Francia), visited Argentina, discovering there a great potential for producing high-quality wines. He then sent enologist Rénaud Poirier to study these regions; tests were run with many vintages and after finishing the 1959 harvest it determined that Mendoza highlands were ideal not only from their rocky ground but fundamentally for its sunny days and cool nights, with a broad thermal range allowing to obtain grapes of great aromatic concentration, body and flavour. It was this way that the same year Robert Jean de Vogué decided to create in Agrelo, Luján de Cuyo, the first branch of Moët & Chandon outside France: Bodegas Chandon. Two hundred years of French heritage plus forty years of experience in Mendoza wines are reflected in every product.

Location
Route 15 km 29 (5509) Agrelo (Mendoza).

Wines
Dos Voces, Latitud 33°, Valmont, Insignia, O_2, Castel, Clos du Moulin, Comte de Beltour.
Sparkling wines: Barón B, Chandon and Mercier

Visits and tasting
With previous notice. February-March-July: Monday-Friday: 9:30, 11:00, 12:30, 14:30 and 16 hs; Saturday: 9:30, 11:00 and 12:30 hs. Rest of the year: Monday-Friday: 10:30, 12:00, 14:30 and 16:00 hs.

Contact
Phone: (54 261) 490-9968
E-mail info@chandon.com.ar
Website:
www.bodegaschandon.com.ar

BODEGAS Y VIÑEDOS EL LAGAR SRL CARMELO PATTI

Purchased in August 1998 by owner Carmelo Patti, carrying out all necessary modifications. The idea was craft manufacturing in limited batches.

Location
San Martín 2614 (5507), Mayor Drummond. Luján de Cuyo (Mendoza)

Wines
Carmelo Patti "Gran Assemblage", Carmelo Patti
Sparkling wines: Carmelo Patti

Visits and tasting
With previous reservation by phone.

Contact
Phone: (54 261) 4981379/ (54 261)155601020

BODEGA ENRIQUE FOSTER

In 2001 Enrique Foster, a U.S. American residing in Spain first tasted an Argentine *Malbec* and this prompted his purchasing of an old vineyard at Luján de Cuyo planted in 1919. Having set up his mind to produce the world's best *Malbec* he studied the most advanced technologiy n California to take it to Mendoza where he built the first plant exclusively dedicated to the elaboration of *Malbec* with gravity flow of must. In its vineyards the new system of conduction by high wires drastically reduced its yield per unit area for a better concentration of *Malbec* flavours.

Location
San Martín 5039 (5507) Luján de Cuyo (Mendoza).

Wines
Enrique Foster Edición Limitada, Enrique Foster Reserva and Ique.

Visits and tasting
No touristic visits are conducted.

Contact
Phone/fax: (54 261) 496-1579 / 1240
E-mail: contact@bodegafoster.com
Website: www.bodegafoster.com

BODEGA ESCORIHUELA

Towards the end of XIX century Don Miguel Escorihuela Gascón sailed from Aragón (Spain) to Argentina at the age of 19. Four years later he bought 42 acres of land, planted vineyards, built a cellar and created one of Mendoza's oldest wine companies. His goal was to achieve top quality wines from choice and care of varieties, elaboration following craft methods and ongoing incorporation of technology. With a team of Argentine professionals and the advice of foreign enologists and technicians this company achieves a high standard of international quality.

Location
Belgrano 1188 (5501) Godoy Cruz (Mendoza).

Wines
Miguel Escorihuela Gascón, Escorihuela Gascón varietales and Familia Gascón varietales

Visits and tasting
Monday through Friday in the wine-bar at the end of the plant tour, with notice in advance.

Contact
Phone (54 261) 424-2282 / 2268 / 2744
Fax (54 261) 424-2857
E-mail: sfacchin@escorihuela.com
cdeonzalez@escorihuela.com
Website: www.escorihuela.com

BODEGAS Y VIÑEDOS O. FOURNIER

With the dawn of a new Milennium the Spanish family Ortega Gil - Fournier founds a small *boutique* company at the foot of the Andes in La Consulta locality.

Location
Los Indios s/n, between ruta 40 and Ghilardi (5567) Eugenio Bustos (Mendoza)

Wines
A Crux, B Crux and Urban Uco

Visits and tasting
Only with reservation

Contact
Phone: (54 2622) 451088 (54 2622) 451598
E-mail: info@ofournier.com
Website: www.ofournier.com

BODEGA LAGARDE

Founded in 1897 it's one of the few companies appeared with the XIX century boom of wine industry that still preserves craft elaboration. Artillery Capt. Don José Ángel Pereira was responsible for its foundation as he decided to settle in Luján de Cuyo on his return from the Campaign of the Desert. There he built a cellar with thick adobe walls and light mud and cane roofs, which stand unscathed today. In 1975 the Perscamona family purchases the company to produce exclusively high-quality wines. Today it has 218 ha [883 acres] and a 2,450,000 liter [647,292 gal] working capacity.

Location
San Martín 1745 (5507) Mayor Drummond - Luján de Cuyo (Mendoza).

Wines
Semillón 1942, Henry, Lagarde Guarda, Lagarde Clásica and Altas Cumbres
Sparkling wines: Lagarde and Altas Cumbres

Visits and tasting
Monday through Saturday with reservation.

Contact
Phone/fax in Mendoza:
(54 261) 498-0011 / 498-3330
Phone/fax: in Buenos Aires city:
(54 11) 5077-0807
E-mail: info@lagarde.com.ar
Website: www.lagarde.com.ar

BODEGA LA RURAL

Renowned for the high quality of its wines since its very foundation (1885) by Felipe Rutini this company also houses the Wine Museum, the most important of its kind in America- featuring 5,000 pieces (machinery, old carts and tools) reflecting the history of viniculture, allowing visitors to travel back to the rough, artisan beginnings of this industry. Modern technology and French oak casks can be seen in present-day plant supporting the style of these wines. The place has very important enogical and historical relevance, and a visit is crowned at the cask-surrounded tasting room.

Location
Montecaseros 2625 (5515) Coquimbito - Maipú (Mendoza).

Wines
Felipe Rutini, Apartado, Antologías, Colección Rutini, Trumpeter, San Felipe Roble
Sparkling wines: Rutini and Trumpeter

Visits and tasting
Monday through Friday, Sunday and holidays as the finishing of the visit to the Wine Museum, with reservation by phone or e-mail.

Contact
Phone in Mendoza: (54 261) 497-2013.
Fax (54 261) 497-3956
Phone in Buenos Aires city: (54 11) 4343-5224.
Fax (54 11) 4334-4856
E-mail: promocion@bodegalarural.com.ar
Website: www.bodegalarural.com.ar

BODEGAS Y VIÑEDOS LAVAQUE

The founders of this traditional company were Félix Lavaque and Rodolfo Paolucci, in every sector still persisting the quality and commitment to presenting locally and internationally renowned exquisite fine wines. The family has always been present in the wine company, working with the best technology available and contributing as time went by new methods and technics for improvement witn European latest-generation equipment. Today Rodolfo Félix Lavaque with her son Francisco combine a tradition in wine-making with a firm policy of innovation, integration and expansion.

Location
Félix Lavaque: Route 40 km 1046 (4427) Cafayate (Salta)
Bodega Lavaque: Ruta Provincial 165 s/n (5603) Cañada Seca, San Rafael (Mendoza)

Wines
Félix Lavaque, Lavaque Roble, Lavaque Varietales, Rincón Privado, Quara and Cornejo Costas

Contact
Phone Félix Lavaque: (54 3868) 421709
Bodega Lavaque: (54 2627) 497044/132.
E-mail: info@lavaque.com
Website: www.vinasdealtura.com

BODEGAS LÓPEZ

An exceptional case in the Argentine vinicultural industry started more than a hundred years ago, it is still today in the hands of the founding family, run by the third and fourth generation under the presidence of Mr. Carlos Alberto López. The wise combination of ancestral traditions with an ongoing technological updating give their wines a dual condition of of classical and modern. Founder José López Rivas arrived in 1886 from the Algarrobo village in Málaga, Spain. The company's philosophy has always been based on quality, brand and image.

Location
Ozamis 375 (5511) Gral. Gutierrez, Maipú (Mendoza)

Wines
Montchenot, Château Vieux, Casona López, Rincón Famoso, Xero
Sparkling wines: Montchenot and Mont Reims

Visits and tasting
Monday through Friday 9:00 to 17:00. Saturday and holydays 9:30 to 12:30.   Free of charge with guide.

Contact
Phone: (54 261) 497-2406 - Fax (54 261) 4973610
E-mail: lopezmza@bodegaslopez.com.ar; lopezbue@bodegaslopez.com.ar
Website: www.bodegaslopez.com.ar

BODEGA LUIGI BOSCA

This Mendoza company belonging to the Arizu family has an extensive trajectory in the vinicultural industry that arises from the thorough work in vineyards and permanent experimentation with different grape varieties exposed to diverse climates, soils and heights. Now in its fourth generation the company underwent an extensive growth process in the local market and an important penetration in the European market with international expansion. The tour includes the astounding *Wine's Via Crucis* by Mendoza artist Hugo Leytes, formed by 14 high-relief murals narrating the arrival of the first European immigrants who started wine industry in Argentina.

Location
San Martín 2044 (5507) Mayor Drummond - Luján de Cuyo (Mendoza).

Wines
Finca Los Nobles, Gala 1 and Gala 2, Luigi Bosca Reserva, Finca La Linda.
Sparkling wines: Boheme, Luigi Bosca and Finca La Linda

Visits and tasting
Monday through Saturday in the Visitor Center with reservation.

Contact
Phone in Mendoza (54 261) 498-1974 - Fax (54 261) 498-2086
Phone in Buenos Aires city (54 11) 4331-2206
Fax (54 11) 4331-8863
E-mail:luigibosca@luigibosca.com.ar;
aroman@luigibosca.com.ar
Website: www.luigibosca.com.ar

BODEGA Y VIÑEDOS MAURICIO LORCA

The plant is located at little more than 100 km [62.5 mi] from Mendoza city, in Valle del Uco. Its corporate view includes the idea of producing varietal wines full of typical character and personality paying homage to Mendoza's generous nature which combines thermal range, the virtues of soil and a gentle climate. As a concept a 6,850 plants per hectare [1,692 per acre] was designed to get the best raw material and thus make red wine of high concentration and complexity. It's in the aim of this company to set a trend in production of intense wines that show the potential of Argentine *terroir*.

Location
Callejón Troilo s/n (5565) Vista Flores, Tunuyán (Mendoza).

Wines
Ópalo, Lorca Fantasía and Lorca Poético.

Visits and tasting
No touristic visits are conducted.

Contact
Phone/fax: (54 261) 496-1579 / 1240
E-mail: info@opalowines.com
Website: www.opalowines.com

BODEGA MONTEVIEJO

Seven friends gather in Argentina to plant vineyards together in an exceptional estate harmonically integrated into a gorgeous environment. Ditches, aqueducts, dams, underground wires. In 1998 enologists Michel Rolland and the late Jean-Michel Arcaute with Catherine Péré-Vergé, owner of Château Montviel in Pomerol; Laurent Dassault owner of Saint-Emilion; Bertrand Otto, agent of Compagnie Vinicole E. Rothschild; and Bertrand Cuvelier. They divided the *terroir* in seven plants, calling the set "Le Clos de los Siete" [The Seven's Cellar].

Location
Clodomiro Silva s/n (5565), Vista Flores, Tunuyán (Mendoza)

Wines
Val de Flores, Clos de los Siete, Lindaflor, Petit Fleur and Festivo

Visits and tasting
Consult.

Contact
Phone: (54 2622) 422054
E-mail: bodegamonteviejo@monteviejo.com
Website: www.monteviejo.com

BODEGA NAVARRO CORREAS

The history of this traditional company dates back to year 1798 when Juan de Dios Correas planted the first seeds in Mendoza land. Don Juan de Dios was an important politician who fought alongside General San Martín for Argentine independence, as well as in the campaigns to free Chile and Peru from Spanish domain. In 1974 Don Edmundo Navarro Correas decided to start manufacturing wines under hos own name and with his uncle Julián Correas, a born innovating enterprise began this new stage, thus becoming one of Argentina's most prestigious companies. C.I.N.B.A. S.A. is in charge of product commercialization while elaboration continues the familiar tradition of Edmundo Navarro Correas's nephews.

Location
San Francisco del Monte s/n (5501), Godoy Cruz (Mendoza)

Wines
Ultra, Gran Reserva, Colección Privada, Finca Dolores and Los Arboles
Sparkling wines: Navarro Correas.

Visits and tasting
Monday, Wednesday and Friday 10:00, 12:00 and 15:00 with reservation.

Contact
Phone: (54 261) 4315987 / 9
E-mail: contacto@ncorreas.com
Website: www.ncorreas.com

BODEGA NIETO SENETINER

The history of this company dates back to 1888 when two families of Italian immigrants arrived at Luján de Cuyo with the vision of founding their first company. In 1960 its shareholders change, its definitive name is formed and it experiences deep growth that allows expansion of its premises, thus originating a new stage. Today its plant has advanced technologies such as measurement of relative humidity in the different layers of the soil and drop irrigation integration. It boasts of 300 ha [1,215 acres] of strategically located vineyars covering the principal needs of high-quality grape supply for the developments of their products.

Location
Guardia Vieja s/n (5507) Vistalba - Luján de Cuyo (Mendoza).

Wines
Cadus, Nieto Senetiner Bonarda, Don Nicanor, Nieto Senetiner Varietales , Benjamín Nieto.
Sparkling wines: Nieto Senetiner

Visits and tasting
Visits are free of charge, Monday through Sunday and include tasting. Special tasting in the vineyards is with reservation and charged.

Contact
Phone: (54 261) 498-0315 / 4027
E-mail: amantesdelvino@nietosenetiner.com.ar
Website: www.nietosenetiner.com.ar

BODEGA PALO ALTO

A family company formed by professionals who combined their successful experience in corporate management with their love for the land of Mendoza and their passion for the nobility of the produce of grapevine, who have the major goal of making a vision come true: committin to reaching the ultimate expresion of grapevine by transforsming it exclusively into top quality wines.

Location
Videla Aranda 502 (5517), Cruz de Piedra. Maipú (Mendoza)

Wines
Palo Alto Reserva, Coirón, Satomi

Visits and tasting
Monday through Friday, 10:00 to 16:00

Contact
Phone: (54 261) 499-0407
E-mail: bodega@vinarium.com.ar
Website: www.vinarium.com.ar

BODEGAS Y VIÑEDOS ROCA S.A.

Always based on a same policy this company was built on quality pillars adding all the technology available from science to winemaking tradition. Forebears of Alfredo Roca—today president of this company—came to San Rafael from Italy and Spain with the aim of dedicating themselves to the cultivation of grapevine to obtain high quality wines. As an enologist he absorbed this culture and focused on the elaboration of prestigious wines. Today this company is being run by the fourth generation of this family, working with the same passion and commitment of its beginnings.

Location
Provincial Route 165 and La Pichana street (5603), Cañada Seca (Mendoza)

Wines
Roca Exclusivo, A. Roca Reserva and A. Roca Varietales

Visits and tasting
Monday through Friday

Contact
Phone: (54 2627) 497194 / 497250
E-mail: roca@rocawines.com
Website: www.rocawines.com

BODEGA RUCA MALÉN

Its owners are Jean-Pierre Thibaud, with a vast experience in the wine business thanks to his 10 years presidency of Bodegas Chandon in Argentina, and Jacques-Louis de Montalembert, also with a long viticultural history since his birth in the Bordeaux area in France. Ruca Malen manufactures limited batches of wine from exclusive, selected vineyards.

Location
National Route 7 km 1 (55 59), Agrelo, Luján de Cuyo (Mendoza)

Wines
Kinien, Ruca Malen, Yaunquén

Visits and tasting
Monday through Friday, and Saturday 10:00 to 12.30.

Contact
Phone: (54 261) 4541236
E-mail: mespinola@bodegarucamalen.com
Website: www.bodegarucamalen.com

BODEGAS SALENTEIN

This company's facilities are located at more than 1,200 m [3,937 ft.] above sea level at the foot of the Andes, surrounded by vineyards. Its plant is shaped like a cross, each one of its four naves being a small cellar, all converging into a central amphitheater where they share the fractioning room.

Location
Route 89 and Elías Videla s/n (55 60), Los Árboles, Tunuyán (Mendoza)

Wines
Primus, Salentein Roble, Finca El Portillo.

Visits and tasting
Tuesday through Saturday. Free of charge with guide.

Contact
Phone in Mendoza: (54 261) 4238514
Fax: (54 261) 4238565
Phone in Buenos Aires city: (54 11) 4131-1100
Fax: (54 11) 4134-1199
E-mail:info@bodegasalentein.com
Website:www.bodegasalentein.com

BODEGA SÉPTIMA

Séptima is the new plant of Codorníu, a Spanish group dedicated to the manufactured to high quality wines and sparkling wines, a leader in the international market. In Spanish "Séptima" means "seventh" in the female form [corresponding to the gender of the Spanish word for a winemaking plant], seven being a lucky number in Latin culture and the ordinal corresponding to the resting day in the week.

Location
National Route 7, km 6.5 (5509) Agrelo, Luján de Cuyo (Mendoza)

Wines
Séptima Reserva, Séptima Varietales y Bivarietales
Sparkling wines: María Codorníu

Visits and tasting
Monday through Friday, with reservation.

Contact
Phone: (54 261) 498-5164
E-mail: codorniu.arg@codorniu.com
Website: www.bodegaseptima.com.ar

BODEGA TERRAZAS DE LOS ANDES

Located in the heart of Perdriel at the foot of the Andes, XIX craft tradition is combined with modern technology, creating a perfect balance between past and present. With this goal an old majestic building erected in 1898 was restored in 1996. Terrazas de los Andes is a company whose concept synthesizes the benefit of height to achieve wines of unique quality. Each variety is grown on a terrace of a given height designed to achieve its best expression of aroma and flavour: in Perdriel terraces at 980 m [3,215 ft] the *Cabernet sauvignon* reaches its optimum ripening point. The *Malbec* in Vistalba, at 1,067 m [3,500 ft], the *Chardonnay* in valle de Tupungato at 1,200 m [3,937 ft], and the *Syrah* in Cruz de Piedra at 800 m [2,625 ft]. At the Guest House it's possible to enjoy a different stay and live the captivating world of wine.

Location
Thames and Cochabamba (5509), Perdriel, Luján de Cuyo (Mendoza)

Wines
Cheval des Andes, Afincado, Terrazas Reserva and Terrazas Varietales

Visits and tasting
Monday through Friday, with reservation

Contact
Phone in Mendoza: (54 261) 488-0058
Phone in Buenos Aires city:(54 11) 4121-8000/ 4121-8097
E-mail: info@terrazasdelosandes.com
Website:www.terrazasdelosandes.com

BODEGAS TRAPICHE

Founded in 1883 by Tiburcio Benegas, an outstanding winemaker also known for his forays in Mendoza province's politics and economy. In 1970 Trapiche was purchased by the Pulenta family, traditional winemakers from the Cuyo region who drove its growth with important investment in facilities and vineyards. Trapiche eventually became one of the most important wine exporters in Argentina in quality and quantity, today directly reaching more than forty countries. The facilities were revamped in this decade, leaving as a result a perfect match between traditional craftsmanship and the most modern production technology.

Location
Mitre s/n (5522), Coquimbo, Maipú (Mendoza)

Wines
Iscay, Gran Medalla, Medalla, 120 años, Fond de Cave, Colección Roble, Origen, Broquel, Varietales, Septiembre and Astica
Sparkling wines: 1883 Cuvée and 1883

Visits and tasting
Not conducted.

Contact
Phone: (54 261) 520-7210
E-mail:lyofe@trapiche.com.ar
Website: www.trapiche.com.ar

BODEGA FAMILIAR VIÑA EL CERNO

Being a very small family company, varietals are elaborated with the very same technology used by our ancestors, love and dedication. Touring the cellars it is possible to appreciate the magic of the old and the purity of craft. The place was recovered by María Ester Carra and Pedro José Martínez where besides wine production they receive tourists and teach them to understand their wines' *terroir* and to taste them while finding their special message.

Location
Carril Moreno 631 (5513), Coquimbito, Maipú (Mendoza)

Wines
Antiguo, Sexta Viña, Viña El Cerno varietales, Wayna varietales
Sparkling wines: Viña El Cerno

Visits and tasting
Monday through Saturday

Contact
Phone: (54 261) 4964929
E-mail: elcerno@lanet.com.ar
Website: www.elcerno.com.ar

BODEGAS Y CAVAS DE WEINERT

Founded in 1975 by Don Bernardo C. Weinert in Luján de Cuyo. Born in a small German colony in southern Brazil, fascinated by the world of wine he decided to create his own company in Argentina with an unconditional philosophy: producing high quality wines. He studied the climate, soil and grapevines, restored a building purchased in 1974, brought the latest wine-making technology of that day and recruited renowned enologists. He produced wines famous among prestigious tasters all over the world.

Location
San Martín 5923 (5505), Chacras de Coria, Luján de Cuyo (Mendoza).

Wines
Weinert Estrella, Cavas de Weinert, Weinert Varietales, Carrascal

Contact
Phone: (54 261) 4960721
E-mail: info@bodegaweinert.com
Website: www.bodegaweinert.com

CAVAS DE SANTOS

Engineer Santos Beck started as an enthusiastic wine collector in 1998. As years went by his career got him closer to vinicultural regions by generating a strong bond with land, wines and people. In 1999 he started working in vineyard selection and manufacturing small batches of high-quality wine. Today, with a specialized technical team he achieved a presence of his wines in the national marketplace and a permanent, increasing penetration in the international market. This company's concept is about introducing the consumer into the wine culture by highlighting the potential of the Mendoza and San Juan microregions.

Location
Roque Sáenz Peña 5516 (5509), Vistalba, Luján de Cuyo (Mendoza)

Wines
Cavas de Santos Gran Reserva, Cavas de Santos Línea Clásica, Moscatel de Alejandría

Visits and tasting
Directed tasting in commercial offices in Buenos Aires city (Perú 457 5º C).

Contact
Phone/fax: (54 11) 4343-3762/ 4342-4367
E-mail: info@cavasdesantos.com.ar
Website: www.cavasdesantos.com.ar

CAVAS ROSELL BOHER

Alejandro Martínez Rosell is continuing the family tradition of sparkling wines under the motto of manufacturing the best product. Several carefully selected "clones" of *Pinot Noir* y *Chardonnay* are cultivated in Mendoza's best areas. Different basic wines obtained from these allow for a refined later selection with the aim of obtaining the desired complexity in the definitive blend or *cuvée*. The *méthode Champenoise* from the French region of Champagne adopted by this company ensures the highest results in the quality of such wines. Limited batches guarantee the customized care required by artisan production.

Location
Pueyrredón 1210 (5528) Chacras de Coria, Luján de Cuyo (Mendoza)

Wines
Casa Boher, Oveja Negra and Viña de Narváez
Sparkling wines: Rosell Boher and Casa Boher

Contact
Phone/Fax: (54 261) 496-1715
E-mail: info@rosellboher.com
Website: www.rosellboher.com

CHAKANA

Founded in the year 2002 with the purchase of a 300 ha [1,215 acres] estate already planted with 85 ha [344 acres] of 30 year old vineyards. The plant was built in that year in the same lot with the aim of manufacturing single vineyard, estate wines.

Location
Provincial Route N° 15 km 34 (5507), Luján de Cuyo (Mendoza)

Wines
Estate Selection, Reservas and Varietales

Visits and tasting
With reservation.

Contact
Phone: (54 261) 410-6002
E-mail: info@chakanawines.com.ar
Website: www.chakanawines.com.ar

DOMINIO DEL PLATA WINERY

This company is a family project by Susana Balbo (enologist) and Pedro Marchevsky (vineyard grower) who started a project of their own in 1999 as the product of their need for an individual expression of their love and dedication to their disciplines. For this goal they leased premises in other companies' plants in the Luján de Cuyo area. Thanks to sustainable growth they decided to build a new plant in 2001. It has a simple yet unique design with the aim of elaborating personal wines, its inlet has a rolling band for selection of bunches before removal of twigs and pressing.

Location
Cochabamba 7801 (5507) Agrelo, Luján de Cuyo (Mendoza).

Wines
BenMarco, Susana Balbo, Críos de Susana Balbo

Contact
Phone: (54 261) 498-6572/2934
E-mail: info@dominiodelplata.com.ar
Website: www.dominiodelplata.com.ar

FABRE-MONTMAYOU / DOMAINE VISTALBA

Company owner Hervé Joyaux Fabre was born in Bordeaux (France), a member of a family with a long track record in the city's wine business. He came to Mendoza in 1992, attraction to Argentine *Malbec* and New World wines being immediate. His vision drives him to purchase old *Malbec* vineyards planted in 1908 and build a French-style *Château*. His passion and *savoir faire* will do the rest: conceive high quality wines of international prestige.

Location
Roque Saenz Peña s/n (5509) Vistalba, Luján de Cuyo (Mendoza)

Wines
Grand Vin, Grande Reserve, Varietales, Phebus and Trilogie

Visits and tasting
Monday through Friday. Free of charge with guide

Contact
Phone: (54 261) 498-2330
E-mail: info@bodegasdomainevistalba.com.ar
Website: www.domainevistalba.com

FAMILIA CASSONE

The plant project is the work of Eduardo Cassone and his sons Eduardo José, Martín and Federico, inheritors of the pioneering spirit of Roberto Cassone, who began his vinicultural activity in Mendoza in the 1950s with a small plant in Junín department, bequeathing his son Eduardo his passion for the *terroir*.

Location
Terrada and Anchorena s/n (5507), Mayor Drummond, Luján de Cuyo (Mendoza)

Wines
Obra Prima, Finca La Florencia, Madrigal

Visits and tasting
With previous notice.

Contact
Phone: (54 261) 423-3203
E-mail: bodegacassone@familiacassone.com.ar
Website: www.familiacassone.com.ar

FAMILIA ZUCCARDI

This company was founded by Alberto Zuccardi who created an irrigation system fitting the characteristics of this area. His passion for viniculture led him to broaden the culture acquired in 1963 and start building a plant in 1968. Techonlogy is combined with craft in wine-making processes: the company has 650 ha [2,631 acres] of vineyards in two farms where wine cult is the synthesis of a working culture shared by more than 500 people. The plant has an important enological structure from its modern technology as well as its storage capacity (15.000.000 liters [3,963,012 gal]).

Location
Provincial route 33 km 7.5 (5531) Fray Luis Beltrán, Maipú (Mendoza)

Wines
Zuccardi Zeta, Zuccardi Q, Malamado, Santa Julia Magna, Santa Julia Roble and Santa Julia Varietales.
Sparkling wines: Santa Julia

Visits and tasting
Every day in the week. Lunch with reservation.

Contact
Phone: (54 261) 4410000.
Fax: (54 261) 4410010
E-mail: info@familiazuccardi.com
Website: www.familiazuccardi.com

FINCA FLICHMAN S.A.

In 1873, the company's first vineyards and plant are established in Barrancas, Maipú region, province of Mendoza. In 1910, the Flichman family re-inaugurates it under their own name: Finca Flichman. A pioneer and visionary was don Sami Flichman who developed the first vineyards in a gorge long ago excavated by Mendoza river. Currently the facilities preserved, restored and expanded by the Sogrape group, equipped it with the most recent vinification technology: double-casing stainless steel tanks with automated temperature control for cold fermentation and small casks of French and American oak.

Location
Munives 800 (5517) Barrancas, Maipú (Mendoza)

Wines
Dedicado, Paisaje de Barrancas, Paisaje de Tupungato, Caballero de la Cepa, Finca Flichman Varietales.

Visits and tasting
Wednesday through Sunday. Free of charge with guide.

Contact
Phone: (54 261) 497-2039
E-mail: marketing@flichman.com.ar
Website: www.flichman.com.ar

FINCA LA ANITA

This enterprise dates back to the early '90s, by the brothers Manuel and Antonio Mas. With a unique production model the quality obtained is matchless.

Location
Calle Cobos s/n (5509) Agrelo, Luján de Cuyo (Mendoza)

Wines
Finca La Anita, Finca, Luna, Cuarto de Milla.

Visits and tasting
Not conducted

Contact
Phone: (54 261) 490-0255
E-mail: info@fincalaanita.com
Website: www.fincalaanita.com

FINCA SOPHENIA

Roberto Luka, inspirator and main shareholder of Finca Sophenia has a well-documented trajectory in the world of wine. He was General Director of one of the major exporting producers in his country, now he is President of Wines of Argentina. The internationally prestigious French enologist Michel Rolland has been accompanying this enterprise as adviser since the first vinification exercise. During 2003 this company recruited enologist Matías Michelini, with a successful track record in high-quality wine.

Location
Provincial Route 89 km 12 (5575) Los Árboles, Tupungato (Mendoza)

Wines
Finca Sophenia, Altosur

Visits and tasting
Not conducted

Contact
Phone: (54 2622) 489680
E-mail: consultas@sophenia.com.ar
Website: www.sophenia.com.ar

JACQUES & FRANÇOIS LURTON

Jacques and François Lurton belong to a great vinicultural family from Bordeaux. In 1988 they found the namesake company with the aim of manufacturing wine from different parts of the globe. In 1992 they came to Argentina to advise domestic companies. Years later they purchased 220 ha [891 acres] in Mendoza starting to produce wine in their own plant based on the idea that it's possible to make good wine in any region where grapevines grow in normal conditions, this way creating a wide range of wines from the Old and New World.

Location
Provincial route 94 km 21 (5565) on the way to the Historical Apple Tree, Vista Flores, Tunuyán (Mendoza).

Wines
Gran Reserva: Chacayes, Piedra Negra and Gran Lurton, Lurton Reserva and Lurton Varietales

Visits and tasting
Basic tasting free of charge with previous appointment. Other tasting with charge, the visitor choosing the wines.

Contact
Phone/fax: (54 261) 492067/78
E-mail: comercial@bodegalurton.com
Website: www.bodegalurton.com

NORTON

Edmund James Palmer Norton, an English engineer, is hired in Argentina for the building of the railway to join Mendoza with Chile. Towards 1889 he settles in the Andean province, founding in 1895 the first company of the region in the Perdriel district in the Luján de Cuyo department. He imports grapevines from France, entirely dedicated to viticulture. He dies in 1944, still remembered for his nobility and warmth. Years went by, the company being purchased in 1989 by Austrian businessman Gernot Langes Swarovski. Today his son Michel is developing an important technological and culture project with a team of professionals.

Location
Provincial Route 15 km 23 50 (5509) Perdriel, Luján de Cuyo (Mendoza)

Wines
Privada, Reserva, Malbec D.O.C., Varietales Roble, Varietales Jóvenes, Bivarietales, Clásico
Sparkling wines: Cosecha Especial and Extra Brut
Perdriel: Centenario and Colección

Visits and tasting
Monday through Friday de 9:00 a 17:00. Free of charge with guide.

Contact
Phone: (54 261) 490-9700
E-mail: norton@norton.com.ar
Website: www.norton.com.ar

RJ VIÑEDOS

Driven by his passion for wine, in 1998 Raúl V. Jofré decided to found this company that has 60 ha [243 acres] in Valle del Uco. Its vineyards develop in a land of remarkable purity, free of pollution. The scant volume of precipitation per year also contributes to rendering any kind of treatment practically unnecessary. The goal of this enterprise is to create its own style of wines that represent the unique characteristics of the *terroir* and in this context achieve the top expression of the fruit, corresponding to the rich contribution of wood. This company is dedicated to the production of high-quality wines in limited batches.

Location
Calle Terrada 2400 (5509) Perdriel, Luján de Cuyo (Mendoza)

Wines
Varietales de Guarda [*varietals for keeping*] and Premium

Visits and tasting
Tuesday, Thursday and Saturday with reservation.

Contact
Phone in Mendoza: (54 261) 424-0790
Phone in Buenos Aires city: (54 11) 4827-5580.
Fax (54 11) 4827-5248
E-mail: rjvinedos@rjvinedos.com
Website: www.rjvinedos.com

VIÑA COBOS S.A.

This project was born in 1998 when the owners, three enologists, collaborated with the Dolium company. First vinifications were done there, with growth they started on their path to independence

Location
Cobos 6445 (5509) Perdriel, Luján de Cuyo (Mendoza)

Wines
Cobos, Bramare, Cocodrilo, Lagarto, El Felino

Visits and tasting
Not conducted.

Contact
Phone: (54 261) 490-0226
E-mail: info@vinacobos.com
Website: www.vinacobos.com

VIÑA DOÑA PAULA S.A.

Viña Doña Paula was founded in 1997 in the Ugarteche area in Luján de Cuyo highlands and Tupungato, at the foot of the Andes. Doña Paula offers a new concept in wine business in Argentina with wines manufactured by New World standards and potencing their typically Argentine character.

Location
Poliducto YPF s/n (5509) Ugarteche (Mendoza)

Wines
Selección de Bodega, Doña Paula Estate, Los Cardos

Visits and tasting
Available.

Contact
Phone: (54 261) 498-4410
E-mail: info@donapaula.com.ar
Website: www.donapaula.com.ar

SALTA

BODEGAS Y VIÑEDOS NANNI

In 1885 Pietro Nanni came from Rosciolo, a small village in central Italy, to settle in Cafayate. In 1897 he founded a small family company, in 1905 purchasing the 11,000 ha [44,534 acres] Chimpa state in the privileged valley of Cafayate. After Pietro's demise in 1935 two of his children, Benjamín and Pedro Nanni walked on his footsteps by implanting wines, building a new plant and making forays into animal husbandry and spice production. In 1964 the estate of Benjamín Nanni took over the company; in 1986 his youngest son José Eduardo gets fully involved with an innovating project: taking advantage of exceptional natural conditions offered by the special microclimate in San José de Chimpa estate to produce organic wines.

Location
Silverio Chavarria 151 (4427), Cafayate (Salta)

Wines
Nanni Varietales Orgánicos

Visits and tasting
Monday through Friday 8:00 to 12:00 and 14:00 to 18:00.

Contact
Phone: (54 3868) 421527
E-mail: bodegananni@salnet.com.ar
Website: www.bodegananni.com

BODEGA DOMINGO HERMANOS

In the heart of Calchaquí Valleys, Cafayate, in the province of Salta, privileged by the fertility of its lands and a unique microclimate it has been producing one of Argentina's best wines since late XX century. Domingo Hermanos, continues the noble winemaking tradition, consolidating today as a modern producer yet with a tradition, growing technified but without forgetting that it makes a craft product. A company with rich past and family tradition solidly projecting to the future based on a clear objective: maintaining excellence in wine production starting at the vineyards through every productive step at plant, ending in every consumer's palate.

Location
Nuestra Señora del Rosario s/n (4427), Cafayate (Salta)

Wines
Palo Domingo, Rupestre, Domingo Molina y Finca Domingo.

Contact
Phone: (54 3868) 421-2225 / (54 11) 4201- 6021.
E-mail: bodega@domingohermanos.com
Website: www.domingohermanos.com

BODEGAS ETCHART
PERNOD RICARD ARGENTINA

The history of Etchart company dates back to 1850, when forebears of the Etchart family started their vinicultural activity in the Cafayate area in Salta. Its vineyards located in La Florida farm purchased in 1938 by Arnaldo Etchart. Famous for its *Torrontés* which by the late '80s impacted wine writer Robert Joseph whose comments stunned the world. Currently Etchart belongs to the French group Pernod Ricard and has the world's highest vineyards at 1,700 m [5,577 ft] above sea level on the Precordillera.

Location
National Route 40 km 1047 (4427), Valle de Cafayate (Salta)

Wines
Arnaldo B, C. Rosa, Ayres de Cafayate and Etchart Privado Varietales

Visits and tasting
Monday through Friday and Saturday. Free of charge, with a guide.

Contact
Phone: (54 3868) 421529
E-mail: etchart@prargentina.com.ar
Website: www.vinosetchart.com

BODEGAS Y VIÑEDOS SAN PEDRO DE YACOCHUYA

The first grapevines were planted in 1913 by the Plaza Navamuel family. The Etchart family purchased the estate in 1986; redesigning and modernizing the headquarters and building the plant. Touristic and technical visits are attended by María Cecilia y Marcos Etchart. Since 1988 Michel Rolland the prestigious enologist has been collaborating with Arnaldo Etchart, specializing in production of red wines.

Location
Finca Yacochuya, c.c. nº 1 (4427), Cafayate (Salta)

Wines
Yacochuya, Michel Rolland, San Pedro de Yacochuya, Torrontés

Visits and tasting
With previous notice

Contact
Phone in Salta: (54 3868) 421233
Phone in Buenos Aires city: (54 11) 4312-9466
E-mail: arnaldoetchart@ciudad.com.ar
Website: www.yacochuya.com

SAN JUAN

BODEGA AUGUSTO PULENTA

This old family company, bequeathed through several generations, has tall adobe walls and metal-sheet roof lying on wooden structures of French pitch-pinewood brought to San Juan by railway from Buenos Aires port. The primitive 40,000-liter [10,568 gal] shed eventually grew to 2,000,000 liters [528,401 gal], today equipped with cooling premises, stainless-steel and pneumatic presses, stainless-steel tanks, automated temperature-control systems and other vinification equipment combining techniques from Italian, French, U.S.A. and Argentine industries.

Location
General Acha 988 (5439) San Martín, Valle de Tulum (San Juan)

Wines
Augusto P., Valbona Reserva and Valbona Varietales

Contact
Phone in San Juan (54 264) 420-2553 / 420-2707
Phone in Buenos Aires city (54 11) 4776-6444 / 4334
E-mail: info@augustopulenta.com
Website: www.augustopulenta.com

BODEGAS CALLIA

Located in the Tulum Valley in San Juan beside Mt. Pie de Palo. Vineyards grow at 630 m [2,067 ft] above sea level. The plant was rebuilt keeping the traditional form and incorporating new technology such as steel tanks, modern pneumatic presses and fractioning rooms.

Location
José María de los Ríos and San Lorenzo s/n (5444) Pie de Palo - Caucete (San Juan).

Wines
Callia Magna, Callia Alta and Signos

Contact
Phone in Buenos Aires city: (54 11) 4131-1100
(54 11) 4131-1199
E-mail: info@bodegascallia
Website: www.bodegascallia.com

FINCA LAS MORAS

Its vineyards are located in Valle de Tulum at the foot of the Andes, San Juan province's prime viticultural area at a 630 m [2,067 ft] above sea level. Its height results in ideal conditions for natural development of the grapevine. This area offers an important spectrum of varieties with high concentration and quality that have successfully adapted in a remarkable way to the soil and a desertic climate with broad thermal range and scanty precipitations. The 407 ha [1,006 acre] state basks in a shiny sun, with an ideal climate that renders the use of any chemicals unnecessary for the elaboration. It also houses many mulberry trees [its Spanish namesake] typical of this region, providing shade during the torrid summer and shelter in the mild winters.

Location
Colón and Rawson s/n (5439), San Martín (San Juan)

Wines
Mora Negra, Finca Las Moras Reserva and Finca Las Moras Varietales.

Visits and tasting
Not conducted.

Contact
Phone: (54 264) 497-1031/(54 264) 497-1060
E-mail: danielekkert@fincalasmoras.com
Website: www.fincalasmoras.com

LA RIOJANA

It is a co-operative that succeeded in obtaining ISO 9001 quality certification. It is now implementing HACCP norms and developing a line of certified organic wines. The province's most important wine company, it was built by its present-day proprietors, the son of immigrants from Friule region in Italy.

Location
La Plata 646 (5360), Chilecito (La Rioja)

Wines
Santa Florentina Varietales
Sparkling wines: Brut de Torrontés and Dolce

Visits and tasting
On request by phone.

Contact
Phone: (54 3825) 423150
E-mail: lariojana@lariojana.com.ar
Website: www.lariojana.com.ar

PATAGONIA - NEUQUÉN

BODEGA DEL FIN DEL MUNDO

In 1999 the first harvest of implanted vineyards took place; in 2002 the first of four stages comprised by the project was inaugurated. A modern plant with functional architecture, it has last-generation equipment with stainless-steel facilities and oak casks.. The plant comprises four modules, 190 stainless-steel tanks, 1,000 French and American oak casks with a total capacity of 4,206 million liters [1,111,228 gal] as well as 500,000 bottles storage capacity. Alongside production this company is constantly engaged in original research on the adaptability of new varieties to Patagonian soils, new methods for grapevine conduction, density per unit area, irrigation, etc.

Location
Provincial Route 8 km 9 (8305), San Patricio del Chañar (Neuquén)

Wines
Special Blend, Ventus, Postales del Fin del Mundo, Reserva and Newen

Visits and tasting
10:00 to 16:00 every day

Contact
Phone: (54 299) 485-5004/(54 299)155800414
E-mail: bodegadelfindelmundo@lainversora.com.ar
Website: www.bodegadelfindelmundo.com

FAMILIA SCHROEDER

Owned by a traditional family from Neuquén, this company is located within the viticultural development area "Chañar III Etapa" [*third stage*], north of Argentine Patagonia. During the plant's groundbreaking the remains of a *Titanosaurus* were dug up, it was a plant-eating dinosaur over 15 m [50 ft] long. This event inspired the name "Saurus" for its products. It's possible to tour the facilities every day while watching the elaboration process and see the remains of this place's illustrious dweller.

Location
50 km [31.25 mi] north of Neuquén city on Provincial Route 7, Calle 7 Norte (8305), San Patricio del Chañar (Neuquén)

Wines
Saurus, Saurus Patagonia Select and Familia Schroeder

Visits and tasting
Guided visits and restaurant Monday through Sunday.

Contact
Phone: (54 9299) 155086767 / (54 9299) 155880359
E-mail: info@familiaschroeder.com
Website: www.familiaschroeder.com

NQN, VIÑEDOS DE LA PATAGONIA

By mid-2001 the shareholders of Viñedos de la Patagonia purchased 162 ha [656 acres] in Colonia San Patricio del Chañar, an estate planted with diverse varieties of fine grapes. Today it has a drop irrigation system, different grape varieties, the plant and a team of technicians with a long track record. The aesthetical concept sought for the plant design resulted from the harmonic integration with the Patagonian environment without losing touch with the company's technical needs. The project regarded treatment of liquid and solid industrial residues, building an effluent-treatment plant.

Location
Provincial Route 7 - Calle 15 (8305) San Patricio del Chañar, Añelo (Neuquén)

Wines
Malma Reserva, Malma Varietales, Picada 15

Visits and tasting
Monday through Friday and holidays, contact in advance.

Contact
Phone/fax: (54 299) 443-1069 / 155887801
E-mail: vinpat@vinpat.com.ar
Website: www.vinpat.com.ar

BODEGA INFINITUS

After a first investment in Mendoza with the creation of Bodega Fabre Montmayou, Hervé Joyaux Fabre decided to purchase vineyards and a plant in Patagonia, choosing the unique climate and terroir of Río Negro to make high-quality wines different from those produced in Mendoza. Located in a rustic environment, this plant produces wines where the *connoîsseur* will recognize the citric flavours of *Sémillon*, the elegance of *Chardonnay*, the typical features of Argentine *Malbec*, the body of *Cabernet sauvignon* and the mellow roundness of *Merlot*. Prior to bottling wines are clarified with fresh egg white to ensure perfect clearness without altering their personality and structure.

Location
Ruta 22 and Rajneri (8332), General Roca (Rio Negro)

Wines
Infinitus Gran Reserva, Infinitus Varietales
Sparkling: Infinitus

Contact
Phone: (54 261) 498-2330
E-mail: info@bodegainfinitus.com
Website: www.domainevistalba.com

PATAGONIA - RÍO NEGRO

ESTABLECIMIENTO HUMBERTO CANALE

This company founded in 1904 by the namesake Engineer is one of the world's southernmost vinicultural plants. At 39.2 °S the special climate alternating very cold nights with sunny days constitutes the ideal factor for the cultivation of fine varieties. Four generations after, the company combines the founder's artisan wisdom with state-of-the-art techniques that enable it to produce international quality fine wines. It has a storign capacity of 3,200,000 liters [845,443 gal] more than half of which are kept in vats, barrels and casks of French and American oak.

Location
Chacra 186 (8332) General Roca (Río Negro).

Wines
Marcus Gran Reserva, Humberto Canale Roble, Humberto Canale, Marcus

Contact
Phone in Río Negro: (54 2491) 430415 - Fax (54 2941) 499024
Phone in Buenos Aires city: (54 11) 4307-1506/7990
Fax (54 11) 4362-3436
E-mail: info@bodegahcanale.com; comex@bodegahcanale.com
Website: www.bodegahcanale.com

FINCA DON DIEGO

Well into the Andes, at a 1,505 m [4,938 ft] above sea level, this company produces wines for export in 80 ha [324 acres]. The company name honors both Don Diego Centurión, father and grandfather of current owners and Don Diego Carrizo de Frites who introduced the grapevine in Fiambalá towards 1702. Harmonically with buildings in the area the plant was integrally built with adobe made of its own soil. These walls founded with stone from the Andes, and cane and wooden roof house the best technology for quality vinification. Volcanic sand roofs and the 50 cm [1.64-ft] thick walls ensure a uniquely stable temperature.

Location
Av. de las Américas s/n. National Route N° 60 (5345) San Pedro, Fiambalá (Catamarca)

Wines
Don Diego Reserva and Don Diego Varietales

Visits and tasting
Monday through Friday with phone or e-mail order reservation.

Contact
Phone in Buenos Aires city: (54 11) 4954-6835
Fax (54 11) 4953-8001
E-mail: info@fincadondiego.com; turismo@fincadondiego.com
Website: www.fincadondiego.com

Other producers

We enclose below a list with other Argentine companies, not featured in the preceding section for want of necessary information. However, in order to provide a *Handbook* as complete as possible we include contact information for those who want to know more about them.

Companies in Mendoza

Abril S.A.: bodegaabril@speedy.com.ar
Aconquija de J.A. Furque: graciela-bruno@ar.inter.net
Adunka SA: adunkasa@nysnet.com.ar
Alma 4: alma4@alma4.com
Alto Las Hormigas: vazquez@altolashormigas.com
Alto Perdriel S.A.: bodega@altoperdriel.com.ar
Altocedro: altocedro@nysnet.com.ar
Andean Winieres: agustin.cabral@andeanwineries.com
Antonio Nerviani SA Bodegas y Viñedos: sanerviani@sinectis.com.ar
Antucurá: info@antucura.com
Arturo Bertona: info@montecinco.com.ar
Atilio Avena: atilioavena@speedy.com.ar
Balbi- Mumm: ada@adsw.com
Banfi: ventas@simmetry.com.ar
Baquero 1886: baquero@arnet.com.ar
Benedetti SRL Bodegas y Viñedos: bgabenedetti@infovia.com.ar
Benegas S.A.: info@bodegabenegas.com
Besares Cava: juancarlos@cavabesares.com
Bombal: info@estanciancon.com
Calderón: vinos@cabanascalderon.com.ar
Campo Negro SA: ricardorosell@supernet.com.ar
Carmine Granata Bodegas y Viñedos: bodegacarminegranata@arnet.com.ar
Cavas de Chacra: ocfyasociados@aol.com
Cavas del Conde: cavasconde@infovia.com.ar
Caves de Joulle: cjoulie@arnet.com.ar
Conallbi Grinbreg Casa Agrícola: cg_vinicola@ciudad.com.ar
Cooperativa Vitivinícola Pte. Quintana: quintana@rcc.com.ar
Crotta S.A. Bodegas y Viñedos: crotta@infovia.com.ar
Cruz de Piedra S.A.: bodega@bodegacruzdepiedra.com.ar
Cuarta Generación Cabrini: ivgcabri@infovia.com.ar
Cuchillas de Lunlunta S.A.: malbec@ricardosantos.com
Cuevas del Puma SRL: infobodega@cuevasdelpuma.com
Dolium S.A.: dolium@dolium.com
Don Alberto S.A. Cava: cavasdonalberto@sanmartinmza.com.ar
Don Alejandro: bdonalejandro@infovia.com.ar

Don Bosco: bodegadonbosco@infovia.com.ar
Don Cristóbal: infobodega@doncristobal.com.ar
Duret: info@bodegaduret.com
El Portillo: info@bodegaelportillo.com
Esmeralda: marketing@bodegasesmeralda.com
Establecimientos Baudron: baudronsa@infovia.com.ar
Familia Adrover: adrover@uolsinectis.com.ar
Familia Barberis: mendoza@bodegabarberis.com
Familia Marguery Casa Vinícola: info@marguerywines.com
Fapes Bodegas y Viñedos: fapes@fapes.com.ar
Fecovita Coop. Ltda.: fecovita@fecovita.com.ar; marketing@fecovita.com
Filippo Figari S.A. Bodegas y Viñedos: info@filippofigari.com.ar
Finca Algarbe: info@finca-algarve.com.ar
Finca Don Martino: info@fincasdonmartino.com.ar
Finca La Celia S.A.: info@fincalacelia.com.ar
Finca Urquiza S.A.: videurquiza@sinectis.com.ar
Finca Viña del Golf: info@ricardojuradosa.com.ar
Fincas Andinas S.A.: fincasandinas@fincasandinas.com
Flecha de los Andes Bodegas y Viñedos: p_richardi@uolsinectis.com.ar
Gabutti SA: gabuttisa@infovia.com.ar
Galán: agonzalez@sion.com
Gargantini Bou: wines@gargantinibou.com.ar
Gentile Collins S.A.: bodega@gentilecollins.com
Giaquinta Hnos. SRL: giaquintavinos@ssdnet.com.ar
Goyenechea S.A.: bodega@goyenechea.com
Gruget Bodegas y Viñedos: quirogag@arnet.com.ar
Hacienda Del Plata: info@haciendadelplata.com.ar
Hispano Argentina: enrique@bha.com.ar
Inti Huaco: bodegaintihuaco@infovia.com.ar
J. A. Cicchitti S.A.: inform@bodegacicchitti.com
Jean Rivier e Hijos SRL: bodega@jeanrivier.com
Jesús Carlos Fantelli e Hijos: fantelli@sanmartinmza.com.ar
José Luis Pugni Bodegas y Viñedos: bodegas_pugni@tutopia.com
La Azul S.A.: shirley@slatinos.com.ar
La Carmela Vinícola Cava: champanahom@argentina.com
La Misión: bodega@vinosalfredocatena.com
La Vendimia: vendimia@satlink.com
Lanzarini Bodegas y Viñedos: info@lanzarini.com
Lariviere Yturbe: bodegasly@ciudad.com.ar
Llaver SA: bodegallaver@bodegallaver.com.ar
Los Haroldos S.A.: info@vinasdebalbo.com
Los Parrales S.A.: parrales@slatinos.com.ar
Luis Segundo Correas S.A.: lscorreassa@lanet.com.ar

Mainque: mapucura@nysnet.com.ar
Manuel López López: manuellopezlopez@yahoo.com.ar
Mayol: info@bodegamayol.com.ar
Maza Tonconogy: info@mazatonconogy.com.ar
Medrano Estate S.A.: lvillareal@medranowine.com
Mesidor: californ@rcc.com.ar
Miguel Minni Bodegas y Viñedos:
  miguelminni@vinosminni.com.ar
Miroa SA: miroasa@hotmail.com
Orfila: info@orfila.com.ar
Pacheco Pereda S.A.: Phone: (54 11) 47180232
  Fax: (54 11) 47180232
Pascual Toso Bodegas y Viñedos: Phone: (54 261) 4456674 - Fax: (54 261) 4456674
Pequeña Bodega: ventas@pequeniabodega.com.ar
Pokrajac y Cia. S.A.: pokrajac@ciudad.com.ar
Pulenta Estate: info@pulentaestate.com
Pulmary S.A.: info@pulwines.com
Raíces de Agrelo: info@raicesdeagrelo.com.ar
Robino & Cia.: info@bodegarobino.com
Ruggeri: bodegaruggeri@ciudad.com.ar
Sáenz Briones: mrlalin@saenzbriones.com.ar
Salvador Patti Bodegas y Viñedos:
  vinosmedieval@hotmail.com
San Joaquín: mlmgv@hotmail.com
San Telmo: bodega@cruzdepiedra.com.ar
Santa Ana: avivas@bodega-santa-ana.com.ar
Santa Elena S.A.:
  bodegasantaelena@ciudad.com.ar
Simonassi Lyon Bodegas y Viñedos:
  info@bodegasimonassi.com.ar
Suter SA: gjuri@sutersa.com.ar
Tapiz Bodegas y viñedos: tapiz@tapiz.com.ar
Telteca Winery: Phone: (54 2623) 494132 -
  Fax: (542623) 494134
Tierras Altas Vargas Arizu: vinos@vargasarizu.com
Tittarelli: info@vinostittarelli.com.ar
Trivento S.A.: info@trivento.com
Vinecol S.A.: info@vinecol.com.ar
Vinorum: vinorum@nysnet.com
Viña Amalia : fincamalia@nysnet.com.ar
Viña Maipú S.A.: vinamaipu@arnet.com.ar
Viñas de Barrancas: info@vinasdebarrancas.com
Viñas de Euzkadi: ingortiz@supernet.com.ar
Viñedos Los Maitenes S.A.: info@losmaitenes.com
Vita Mediterránea S.A.: vitamediterranea@nysnet.com.ar
Vollmer: moyanovm@slatinos.com.ar

Companies in San Juan

Antigua Bodega: bodegaschirino@arnet.com.ar
Arenas: arenas@infovia.com.ar
Bórbore: info@bodegasborbore.com
Cavas de Zonda S.A.:
  cavasdezonda@uolsinectis.com.ar
Cordero Hnos.:Phone: (54 264) 4222330 / 4222346
  Fax:(54 264) 4222330
Don Doménico: bodegadondomenico@infovia.com.ar
Duilio Clodomiro Graffigna:
  fincadonduilio@infovia.com.ar
Fabril Alto Verde S.A. Bodegas y Viñedos:
  altoverde@arnet.com.ar
Finca La Escondida: Phone: (54 264) 971031 /
  971060 - Fax: (54 264) 971031
Finca La Sylvia: sssj@petersenthieleycruz.com.ar
Graffigna: graffigna@adsw.com

Horacio Nesman S.A. Bodegas y viñedos:
  vinosnesman@infovia.com.ar
Miguel Ángel Más Champagnera:
  miguelmas@infovia.com.ar
Millás Hnos. Bodegas y Viñedos:
  analiamillas@bodegasmillashnos.com.ar
Morchio & Meglioli SA: emorchio@ciudad.com.ar
Putruele Hnos.: bodega@putruele.com.ar
Resero SA: Phone: (54 264) 4911206 / 4911071
  Fax: (54 264) 4911206
Tierras del Huarpe: tierrasdelhuarpe@uolsinectis.com.ar
Viñas de Segisa Bodegas y Viñedos:
  segisa@saxsegisa.com.ar

Companies in Salta

Antigua Bodega La Banda:
  info@vasijasecreta.com
Colomé S.A.: bodega@bodegacolome.com
El Esteco: sreal@elesteco.com.ar
Finca El Recreo: ssarabia@pfrias.com.ar;
  elrecreo@salnet.com.ar
Tacuil: vinosdealtura@uolsinectis.com.ar

Companies in Catamarca

Cabernet de los Andes S.A.: postmaster@vicien.cyt.edu.ar
Elías J. Saleme S.A.: bodegasaleme@yahoo.com.ar

Companies in La Rioja

Anguinan S.A. Bodegas y Viñedos:
  bodegasanguinan@bodegasanguinan.com.ar
La Rioja S.A.: bodegalarioja@hotmail.com
San Huberto SA: bodegalarioja@hotmail.com
Valle de La Puerta S.A.:
  jcluscllas@valledelapuerta.com

Companie in Neuquén

Bodega del Añelo : cofruva@speedy.com.ar

Companies in Río Negro

Agrestis S.A.: ventas@bodeaagrestis.com.ar
Estepa: info@bodegasestepa.com
Noemia de la Patagonia: Phone: (54 2941) 115530412

Index of wine cellars

MENDOZA 132
ACHÁVAL-FERRER 132
ALTA VISTA 133
BIANCHI 134
CARMELO PATTI 137
CATENA ZAPATA 135
CAVAS DE SANTOS 159
CHAKANA 161
CHANDON 136
DOMINIO DEL PLATA WINERY 162
DOÑA PAULA S.A. 173
ENRIQUE FOSTER 138
ESCORIHUELA 139
FABRE-MONTMAYOU / DOMAINE VISTALBA 163
FAMILIA CASSONE 164
FINCA FLICHMAN S.A. 166
FINCA LA ANITA 167
FINCA SOPHENIA 168
FOURNIER 140
LA RURAL 142
LAGARDE 141
LAVAQUE 143
LÓPEZ 144
LUIGI BOSCA 145
LURTON 169
MAURICIO LORCA 146
MONTEVIEJO 147
NAVARRO-CORREAS 148
NIETO SENETINER 149
NORTON 170
PALO ALTO 150
RJ VIÑEDOS 171
ROCA S.A. 151
ROSELL BOHER 160
RUCA MALÉN 152
SALENTEIN 153
SÉPTIMA 154
TERRAZAS DE LOS ANDES 155
TRAPICHE 156
VIÑA COBOS S.A. 172
VIÑA EL CERNO 157

WEINERT	158
ZUCCARDI	165
SALTA	**174**
DOMINGO	175
ETCHART	176
NANNI	174
YACOCHUYA	177
SAN JUAN	**178**
AUGUSTO PULENTA	178
CALLIA	179
LAS MORAS	180
LA RIOJA	**181**
RIOJANA	181
PATAGONIA - NEUQUÉN	**182**
BODEGA DEL FIN DEL MUNDO	182
NQN, VIÑEDOS DE LA PATAGONIA	184
SCHROEDER	183
PATAGONIA - RÍO NEGRO	**185**
CANALE	186
INFINITUS	185
CATAMARCA	**187**
DON DIEGO	187
OTHERS PRODUCERS	**188**
Companies in Mendoza	188
Companies in San Juan	189
Companies in Salta	189
Companies in Catamarca	189
Companies in La Rioja	189
Companies in Neuquén	189
Companies in Río Negro	189

Edition: Cecilia Repetti
Design & layout: Jorge Deverill
Transalation: Mariano Moldes
Photography: Juanjo Bruzza
Review: Marcela Russo y Guadalupe Rodríguez

Deposit by Law 11,723.
Total or partial reproduction is prohibited.

ARGENTINE WINE PRACTICAL HANDBOOK
1st. Edition – 1.500 copies
Printed in Latín Gráfica SRL
Rocamora 4161 - Buenos Aires
April 2006

© copyright 2006 by
Editorial Albatros SACI
J. Salguero 2745 5° 51 (1425)
Ciudad Autónoma de Buenos Aires
República Argentina
www.albatros.com.ar
e-mail: info@albatros.com.ar

ISBN-13: 978-950-24-1164-4
ISBN-10: 950-24-1164-1

Special thanks

The authors thank to Mr. Sergio Di Lorenzo, sommelier, for his advice.

The Publisher is grateful to:
Bodega Terrazas de los Andes,
Bodega Animaná,
Bodega Carmelo Patti,
Bodega Finca Sophenia,
Bodega Luigi Bosca,
Bodega Domingo Hnos,
Bodega Ruca Malén,
Bodega Nanni Hnos,
Bodega Cruz de Piedra,
Bodega J&F Lurton,
NQN, Viñedos de la Patagonia,
RJ Viñedos,
Wine store "Azafrán",
because of the photographs that illustrate this book.

The contents included in this book are exclusive responsability of the author. The Publsher's responsability for physical, material and patrimonial damages is completely excluded.

Dengis, Jorge
  Argentine wine : a practical handbook / Jorge Dengis y Maria Fernanda Dengis - 1a ed. - Buenos Aires : Albatros, 2006.
  192 p. ; 14x22 cm. (Manual práctico)

  Traducción: Mariano Moldes

  ISBN 950-24-1164-1

  1. Vitivinicultura. I. Dengis, Maria Fernanda II. Título
  CDD 634.8